Assessing Tax Reform

Studies of Government Finance: Second Series

TITLES PUBLISHED

Assessing Tax Reform

HENRY J. AARON
HARVEY GALPER

Studies of Government Finance

THE BROOKINGS INSTITUTION

WASHINGTON, D.C.

Copyright © 1985

THE BROOKINGS INSTITUTION

1775 Massachusetts Avenue, NW. Washington, D.C. 20036

Library of Congress Cataloging in Publication data:

Aaron, Henry J.
  Assessing tax reform.
  Includes index.
  1. Tax incidence—United States. 2. Income tax—
United States. 3. Taxation—United States. I. Galper,
Harvey, 1937–   . II. Title.
HJ4653.I53A23 1985   336.2′05′0973   84-45979
ISBN 0-8157-0038-5
ISBN 0-8157-0037-7 (pbk.)

THE BROOKINGS INSTITUTION is an independent organization devoted to nonpartisan research, education, and publication in economics, government, foreign policy, and the social sciences generally. Its principal purposes are to aid in the development of sound public policies and to promote public understanding of issues of national importance.

The Institution was founded on December 8, 1927, to merge the activities of the Institute for Government Research, founded in 1916, the Institute of Economics, founded in 1922, and the Robert Brookings Graduate School of Economics and Government, founded in 1924.

The Board of Trustees is responsible for the general administration of the Institution, while the immediate direction of the policies, program, and staff is vested in the President, assisted by an advisory committee of the officers and staff. The by-laws of the Institution state: "It is the function of the Trustees to make possible the conduct of scientific research, and publication, under the most favorable conditions, and to safeguard the independence of the research staff in the pursuit of their studies and in the publication of the results of such studies. It is not a part of their function to determine, control, or influence the conduct of particular investigations or the conclusions reached."

The President bears final responsibility for the decision to publish a manuscript as a Brookings book. In reaching his judgment on the competence, accuracy, and objectivity of each study, the President is advised by the director of the appropriate research program and weighs the views of a panel of expert outside readers who report to him in confidence on the quality of the work. Publication of a work signifies that it is deemed a competent treatment worthy of public consideration but does not imply endorsement of conclusions or recommendations.

The Institution maintains its position of neutrality on issues of public policy in order to safeguard the intellectual freedom of the staff. Hence interpretations or conclusions in Brookings publications should be understood to be solely those of the authors and should not be attributed to the Institution, to its trustees, officers, or other staff members, or to the organizations that support its research.

*For Joseph A. Pechman
our mentor, critic, and friend*

Foreword

PROPOSALS for important changes in the tax laws are coming from many corners of Congress and from the administration. Labeled tax reform by some advocates, tax simplification by others, and less flattering names by opponents, most of these proposals share two important characteristics. They would broaden the base of the personal and corporation income tax by repealing or reducing dozens of special deductions, credits, exemptions, allowances, and exclusions; and they would lower marginal tax rates. These proposals differ significantly, however, and the differences matter greatly for various groups and industries.

While some critics would reform or simplify the present income tax system, others would prefer just to cut it back. They would replace the lost revenues with proceeds from a new source—a value-added tax, a national sales tax, or energy taxes, for example.

Understanding the competing claims of advocates of the various strategies can be bewildering unless one understands the fundamental problems any tax system must confront—how to raise revenues fairly, how to minimize tax-induced losses of economic efficiency, and how to keep rules simple enough for taxpayers to understand and comply with and for administrators to enforce. Not surprisingly, these admirable goals conflict with one another.

In this book, the twentieth in the second series of Brookings Studies of Government Finance, Henry J. Aaron and Harvey Galper help readers make sense of the cacophony of claims about tax reform. They show how each of the major plans relates to elementary principles of taxation. In addition, they present a plan based on the taxation of personal and business cash flow that, in their view, solves the fundamental problems of taxation better than the proposals now embodied in official reports and draft legislation.

The most important contribution of this book, however, is not the verdict it delivers on one tax plan or another. Rather its principal value is in helping readers to think clearly about the difficult issues in designing and maintaining a fair, efficient, and administrable tax system.

Henry J. Aaron is a senior fellow in the Brookings Economic Studies program and a professor of economics at the University of Maryland; Harvey Galper is a senior fellow in the Brookings Economic Studies program. They wish to thank David Bradford, Daniel Halperin, Robert W. Hartman, Donald Kiefer, Jerome Kurtz, Donald Lubick, Paul E. Peterson, Robert D. Reischauer, Alice M. Rivlin, and Emil Sunley for carefully reading and criticizing early drafts. They also are grateful to Harold S. Appelman, Charles R. Byce, and Gail Morton, who provided research assistance; to Gregg Forte, who edited the manuscript; to Carolyn A. Rutsch, who checked it for accuracy; to Kathleen Elliott Yinug, who typed the manuscript; and to Ward & Sylvan, who prepared the index.

The authors especially wish to thank Joseph A. Pechman, not only for his provocative and vigorous discussion of the current manuscript, but even more for his friendship, support, and criticism over many years.

The views expressed here are the authors' alone and should not be ascribed to the persons whose assistance is acknowledged, to the University of Maryland, or to the trustees, officers, or other staff members of the Brookings Institution.

BRUCE K. MACLAURY
President

April 1985
Washington, D.C.

Contents

Assessing Tax Reform

CHAPTER ONE

Why the United States Must Reform Its Tax System

THE U.S. TAX SYSTEM has become a swamp of unfairness, complexity, and inefficiency. The accumulation of credits, deductions, and exclusions designed to help particular groups or advance special purposes conflict with one another, are poorly designed, and represent no consistent policy. The tax system causes investors to waste resources on low-yield investments that carry large tax benefits, while high-yield investments without such benefits go unfunded. The result is a shrunken tax base that requires needlessly high rates on wages, salaries, and other taxable income. Overall the system undermines the faith of citizens that tax burdens are shared fairly. The time has arrived for basic reform.

The case for rewriting our tax laws would be compelling even if revenues were sufficient to pay for government expenditures—but they are not. Even with Draconian reductions in government spending, the deficit cannot be closed unless revenues are also increased. But raising tax rates on the current highly distorted and shrunken tax base will compound the system's inequities and inefficiencies.

While the need to change our tax laws may be obvious, Congress and the American public receive conflicting advice about exactly what to do. The Treasury Department has advanced one plan. Members of Congress have introduced numerous and diverse proposals of their own. In choosing among these and other plans, Congress and the American public will hear opposing and inconsistent testimony from groups representing business, nonprofit organizations, homeowners, the poor, the elderly—indeed almost any organized coalition one can imagine—about the likely consequences of moving in one direction or another.

To help make some sense out of this chorus of claims and counterclaims, this book dispassionately and analytically examines the issues. To begin, this chapter explains why tax reform is necessary. It also indicates the probable magnitude of the tax increases that will be

1

necessary to balance the federal budget. Finally, it provides a road map to the rest of the book that will help readers over some difficult terrain and let them locate topics of particular interest to them.

The Indictment of the Current Tax System

The personal and corporation income taxes (other than payroll taxes to finance social security programs) accounted for 83 percent of federal revenues in 1984.[1] When these taxes are in disrepair, Americans have a serious economic and political problem. And they are indeed in disrepair; a prosecuting attorney would have no difficulty persuading an impartial jury to convict the federal income tax system of gross unfairness, inefficiency, and complexity. The indictment contains several counts.

Distorting Investment

First, the tax system distorts investment. According to one recent study, the effective rate of tax on broad categories of investments ranges from 91.2 percent to −21.5 percent, depending on the type of investment, the source of funds for the investment, the method of finance, and the tax status of the owner.[2] These variations are causing investment decisions to be based on tax considerations instead of economic productivity.

The social costs of such tax-related distortions can be enormous. They divert resources from their most productive uses—those with highest rates of return before taxes—into uses that are less productive but yield higher after-tax returns. The result is reduced national output, lower productivity, and sluggish economic growth. A simple example illustrates how such antisocial consequences can occur.

1. Congressional Budget Office, *Reducing the Deficit: Spending and Revenue Options* (CBO, 1985), p. 53.
2. Mervyn A. King and Don Fullerton, *The Taxation of Income from Capital: A Comparative Study of the United States, the United Kingdom, Sweden, and West Germany* (University of Chicago Press, 1984), p. 244. If one looks at narrow categories of investment, the range is even larger. Furthermore, these estimates refer to tax rates and other economic assumptions valid in 1980. By 1982 legislation had widened still further the already diverse treatment of different forms of investment.

Suppose that type A investments are taxed at 80 percent (that is, 80 percent of their yield is paid in taxes), type B investments are taxed at 40 percent, and type C investments are free of tax. If the investment risks of each are the same, investors will put their money where they earn the most after taxes. If type C investments yield 6 percent before and after tax (that is, they pay the investor 6 cents per year for every dollar invested), how much will the other two investments have to yield in order to attract investors? The answer is that type B investments will have to earn 10 percent before tax (paying a tax of 40 percent on a return of 10 percent leaves a 6 percent after-tax yield), and type A investments will have to earn 30 percent. That means that a type A investment that yields, say, 29 percent before tax will lose out to a type C investment that yields only 6 percent. When tax rules cause investors to select projects yielding 6 cents per dollar invested in place of others yielding 29 cents, the economy as a whole sacrifices 23 cents (nearly four-fifths) of the potential return. Not all misallocations attributable to the tax system are so extreme. But some are worse.

It is even possible for tax rules to make losing investments profitable. The undesirability of a $10,000 investment this year that pays back a total of only $9,000 seems beyond question. But the tax system can make such a project pure gold. This financial alchemy occurs if the cost of the investment is deductible from ordinary income and the return is treated as a long-term capital gain, only 40 percent of which is taxed. For a taxpayer in the 50 percent tax bracket, the cost of the investment is $5,000 because the $10,000 deduction saves the taxpayer $5,000 in taxes. The investment returns $7,200, calculated as follows: 40 percent of the $9,000 capital gain, or $3,600, is taxable at 50 percent, for a tax of $1,800; so the return is $9,000 less tax of $1,800, or $7,200. Thus, after taxes, the investment returned $2,200 more than the after-tax cost of $5,000— a gain of 44 percent. By the quaint and curious—and economically destructive—rules of the U.S. income tax, an investment with a negative before-tax return of 10 percent is transmuted into a bonanza paying a whopping 44 percent after-tax return. Of such rules are tax shelters made.

Not all tax shelter arrangements are so direct as this example would suggest, and some provisions in the tax code serve to limit the gains from such practices. But the net effects of these tax rules are clear: society as a whole loses from less-productive investment even as investors realize a private gain.

Distorting Wages and Salaries

As a second count in the indictment, the tax system distorts compensation. Unlike other income, most fringe benefits, such as health and life insurance, are not part of employees' taxable income. The tax system thereby encourages fringe benefits, even when the cost of those benefits exceeds the amount employees would be willing to pay for them. The result, once again, is waste of scarce economic resources.

Take employer-financed health insurance, for example. Let's say that a unit of health insurance that costs $1 to provide is subjectively worth only 80 cents to an employee. In the absence of taxes, the employee would choose wages rather than health insurance. If the taxpayer is in the 30 percent tax bracket, however, and health insurance premiums are tax free, the worker would choose health insurance because $1 of wages yields only 70 cents after tax, in contrast to the 80 cents of value the worker ascribes to the health insurance. Thus, the tax system induces people to buy fringe benefits, such as health insurance, that they would not otherwise have bought. The decision to buy health insurance means the sacrifice of other goods and services that yield $1 of benefits for every $1 of cost. If both cash wages and the cost of providing health insurance were taxed equally, the worker in the preceeding example would choose cash compensation, because he or she would prefer 70 cents in after-tax cash income to health insurance that would now give a net benefit of only 50 cents (health insurance benefits subjectively worth 80 cents minus the tax of 30 percent levied on the $1 cost of providing the health insurance).

The same problem arises with other fringe benefits such as group legal insurance, child care services, term life insurance, and accident and disability insurance. If one's employer buys these items, there is no tax. If one buys other consumer goods, one must pay for them out of income remaining after taxes have been paid. Recent legislation has increased the attractiveness of tax-free fringe benefits by permitting employers to offer "cafeteria plans," which are packages that allow workers to choose from a menu of benefits.

The waste from the consumption of products or services with low before-tax, but high after-tax, benefits parallels that which arises when money is put into an investment with a relatively low before-tax yield but high after-tax gains. In both cases, the economy as a whole sacrifices opportunities that have a higher social value than the goods or investments actually chosen.

In short, the tax system encourages people to buy commodities indirectly that they would not choose to buy if all consumer goods were treated alike by the tax system. But this is not the end of the story. By narrowing the tax base, the exclusion of fringe benefits necessitates higher tax rates to collect a given amount of revenue, thus adding to the distortions of all economic decisions.

Distorting Saving

The third count would charge the tax system with distorting saving. If income is saved in some forms such as specific kinds of pension and retirement accounts, the funds saved are not included in current taxable income, and both the income and interest earnings on it are taxed only when withdrawn from these accounts. Other forms of saving are not treated so favorably. As a result, people who save the same amount but in different forms face different tax rates.

It is even possible for people to lower their taxes by depositing funds in retirement accounts, but without saving a dime, simply by transferring funds from one account to another. The Bowery Savings Bank of New York used exactly this argument in a full page advertisement in the *New York Times* (June 6, 1984) to solicit new individual retirement accounts:

Were you to shift $2,000 from your right pants pocket into your left pants pocket, you wouldn't make a nickel on the transaction. However, if those different "pockets" were accounts at The Bowery, you'd profit by *hundreds* of dollars.

Setting up an Individual Retirement Account is a means of giving money to yourself. The magic of an IRA is that your contributions to yourself are tax deductible. A New Yorker in the 40 percent tax bracket who gave herself the maximum $2,000 would receive an $800 present at tax time.

The Bowery may be excused for failing to emphasize that the same options were available at competitors that could accept IRA deposits and that residents of the other forty-nine states also qualified. They may also be excused for not pointing out that the same result could be achieved by borrowing the $2,000 for deposit into the IRA or other tax-sheltered account. In each case, taxpayers who save nothing can cut current taxes under a provision promoted as a savings incentive. Again, these and other base-narrowing provisions boost the tax rates needed to raise a given amount of revenue and thereby increase other tax-related distortions.

Penalizing Work

The fourth charge against the current tax system is that it needlessly penalizes work. As shown in the previous counts of this indictment, the numerous exclusions, deductions, and credits not only give rise to inefficiencies but also greatly constrict the tax base. That means that tax rates on wages and salaries, most of which are taxable, must be much higher than they would be if the base were larger. High tax rates on additional earnings, that is, high marginal tax rates, greatly reduce the reward for work.

Complexity

The fifth charge against the tax system is that it is appallingly complex. Some complexity is the unavoidable side-effect of trying to pursue fairness through precise definitions of the individual circumstances that affect ability to pay. More complexity arises from special incentives for particular activities. And still more arises from an effort to prevent these incentives from unduly reducing tax burdens of high-income taxpayers.

The result is a maze of rules and provisions that makes the tax form all but incomprehensible. An entire industry has arisen to sell advice on how to shelter income legally and another to help people fill out their returns. In the business world, success increasingly rests not on innovating, cutting costs, or marketing effectively but on minimizing taxes. Tax rules cause investors to search for tax provisions they can manipulate instead of investments that are socially and economically productive.

Unfairness

The final, perhaps most serious count is that as a result of all of these provisions, the tax system is just plain unfair. Many people suspect that if the tax system is too complex for them to understand, it must be cheating them. And they are usually right, because those who can hire tax experts to plan their affairs do, indeed, avoid taxes that ordinary citizens pay. However, sometimes the unfairness is replaced by economic inefficiency. This can happen when so many people take advantage of a particular tax provision that the rate of return drops, and the investor gets little more than is available on ordinary investments. In such cases the before-tax return on favored investments is driven below that on fully taxed investments, and this difference is a measure of tax-induced inefficiency mentioned earlier. In short, tax distortions always show up as inequity, inefficiency, or some combination of the two.

Most of the special credits, deductions, and exclusions that complicate the tax code have some appeal when viewed in isolation. Most of them were adopted to advance some social or economic purpose that commands widespread support. However, they partially offset each other and taken together produce unrecognized and unintended side effects, bewilder taxpayers, and undermine the faith of ordinary citizens in the laws to which they are subject.

The prosecutor's closing argument would emphasize another aspect of all this unfairness, inefficiency, and complexity: it doesn't have to be that way.

The Deficit Problem

The tax system suffers from more than the structural deficiencies just enumerated. It also produces too little revenue. Deficits of $200 billion or more, stretching into the indefinite future, are certain unless legislative action is taken to cut spending and raise taxes. These deficits are not attributable to a slack economy, and they cannot be cured by economic growth. The simple fact is that the U.S. government is committed to spending more for defense and domestic programs than current taxes can pay for, even with the economy running at full capacity. If the nation slides into another recession before the end of the decade, deficits could easily reach $400 billion or more.

These deficits are objectionable not because they offend some notion of good fiscal housekeeping but because they will injure the economy. Deficits can help spur demand and reduce unemployment when the economy is operating below capacity. They do so by adding more to demand for goods and services through government spending than they withdraw through taxes. But when the economy is operating at high employment, deficits reduce the growth of productive capacity. The process by which this occurs is simple. U.S. businesses and households usually save 7 to 8 percent of net national income each year;[3] if the government budget is balanced, all these savings are available for investments to expand productive capacity at home and abroad. But deficits now in prospect will absorb half to two-thirds of those savings.

The United States can continue to maintain high levels of investment within its borders only by borrowing from abroad. If present trends continue, the United States will become a net debtor to the rest of the world in 1985 or 1986. Any cutback of the inflow of foreign capital—for example, because of an improvement of investment opportunities abroad— could retard markedly the growth of the capital stock located in the United States. But if foreigners continue to invest in the United States, they will receive most of the income, thereby slowing the growth of U.S. income. The only clear offsetting gains to the United States are the taxes collected on this investment income and the benefits to U.S. labor from working with a larger capital stock.[4]

The federal deficit creates additional unnecessary risks. Because they force the federal government to compete for available saving, deficits keep interest rates artificially high. High interest rates discourage expenditures on long-lived assets such as housing and public utility investments, which lose out to investments in shorter-lived assets. They also sustain the overvaluation of the dollar and the resulting U.S. competitive disadvantage in the world market. In addition, high interest rates place particularly heavy burdens on nations with heavy debts, the service of which is tied to U.S. interest rates. The potential inability of debtor nations to pay interest, let alone principal, on these debts periodically threatens to trigger an international financial or banking crisis.

Agreement that something should be done about the deficit is virtually universal, but there is little consensus about what to do. A politically acceptable program to close the deficit might consist of roughly equal parts of spending reductions and revenue increases; in that case, revenues would have to be increased by approximately $100 billion per year by the end of the decade. Deficit estimates change, partly because of revised economic assumptions. The general deficit picture will not change, however, until Congress acts to cut spending and raise taxes.

3. *Survey of Current Business*, vol. 64 (July 1984), tables 1.7 and 5.1.
4. Even this will come at the expense of foreign workers, including those in less developed nations, whose own capital stock will be reduced as foreign saving flows to the United States.

Reforming Taxes or Raising Them

The need both to reform taxes and to expand revenues creates unusual opportunities and special difficulties. The opportunities derive from the urgency of dealing with the deficit and from a bipartisan recognition that any politically acceptable compromise solution must include tax increases. Leading Republicans and Democrats of both houses of Congress have emphasized this point. They recognize that simply increasing tax rates will worsen the distortions and unfairness of the present tax system. The difficulties arise from the fact that the government needs additional revenue promptly, whereas tax reform is controversial and takes time. It is inconceivable that the Congress and administration could design, enact, and implement tax reform in less than two years; with far-reaching changes, the process would likely take much longer.

Cutting the deficit, however, should not be delayed. Each additional year of $200 billion in red ink permanently adds about $20 billion per year to interest outlays and to succeeding years' deficits (at present interest rates). It also keeps interest rates high, with the destructive consequences already discussed.

If the tax base cannot be significantly broadened in the short run, an increase in tax rates is the only other way to raise revenues. Everyone's tax bill could be increased by a fixed percentage. Or rates could be raised in any pattern desired by changing the entire rate schedule. Alternatively, indexing, which counteracts the effects of inflation, could be repealed or suspended; this would allow inflation to increase effective tax rates by gradually pushing taxpayers into higher brackets. Of course, the distributional effects of alternative tax rate increases can differ substantially.

The dilemma is clear. If the nation waits for structural tax reform, the economic damage from the deficits will grow. If tax rates are raised now, tax distortions will worsen, at least until the tax base is reformed. We believe that deficit reduction is urgent and requires short-run action pending longer-term structural reforms. As revenue from structural reforms becomes available, the short-run revenue measures should be scaled back and eventually repealed. In fact, as we shall show in later chapters, reform of the tax base will generate needed additional revenues at rates well below those in current law.

A Map for This Book

Principles of Taxation

Thinking straight about tax reform requires a set of principles, guidelines for an ideal system, against which specific proposals can be evaluated. Because tax rules interact in complex ways, the guiding principles must be clear and consistent. Chapter 2 is devoted to an exploration of a set of tax principles that meets these standards. The three most important rules are that people with equal economic incomes should pay equal taxes, that taxes should distort economic choices as little as possible, and that tax laws should be easy to understand, obey, and enforce.

Chapter 2 shows that there are two broad areas in which the current income tax violates these principles. The first and most widely recognized area is the ever-growing list of exemptions, credits, and deductions through which Congress tries to support such desirable activities as particular business investments, homeownership, and retirement saving. Most activities that receive some kind of tax forgiveness are meritorious and enjoy widespread support. The problem is that tax benefits usually are extraordinarily inefficient; much of the revenue given up does little or nothing to advance the targeted activities. Also, each additional special provision complicates the system, creates opportunities to engage in favored activities only for tax benefits, and adds to the feeling that the tax system is a maze that can be profitably navigated only by the few. Moreover, the process feeds on itself. When the tax law is encumbered with numerous exemptions, no very strong case can be mounted against the addition of yet one more. As the list grows, so do complexity, inefficiency, and inequity.

The second and less well understood area in which the tax law violates the principles of a desirable system is the taxation of capital income. Four problems with the taxation of income from capital are central. The first arises from inflation. The correct calculation of capital income hinges on its accurate measurement in *real* (that is, inflation-corrected) terms. This means that capital gains, depreciation, interest, and inventory cost must all be adjusted for the effects of inflation. The failure of the current income tax to make these adjustments causes serious mismeasurement of these items, as explained in chapter 2.

A second problem in the taxation of capital income arises from the administrative need to base a tax system as much as possible on *realized* (actual) transactions. It is just too difficult for a tax system to measure unrealized capital income, especially changes in the value of untraded assets. A realization-based system leads to reductions in the tax burden on some forms of capital income, because taxpayers can defer the sale of appreciated assets and hence the payment of taxes. Deferring taxes reduces their burden. A lightened burden is, of course, a benefit to those who experience it, but the economic effects on the economy as a whole are harmful because activities that lend themselves to the deferral of taxes are favored over equally productive activities that are taxed currently.

Third, the current income tax imposes heavier burdens on people who wish to save income for later consumption than it imposes on those who consume their income as they earn it. Fourth, the corporation and personal income taxes, taken together, impose heavier tax burdens on activities undertaken by corporations than on similar activities carried out by unincorporated entities.

Unless these four problems are remedied, the tax system will continue to distort investment and consumption decisions; it will continue to encourage transactions that have as their sole or primary justification the reduction of tax liabilities; and it will continue to impose widely different taxes on persons who have the same income.

Current Reform Plans

In reforming the income tax, Congress can attempt to implement the principle that all income should be taxed once per year, or it can move in some other direction. For example, it might decide to tax only consumption or to impose tax on income measured over some period longer than one year. Or it might reduce reliance on direct taxes on individuals and corporations by imposing some kind of national sales tax.

Chapter 3 explains the strengths and weaknesses of three major proposals to return the income tax to the principle that all income should be taxed once per year: the tax plan advanced by the Treasury Department;[5] the "FAIR" tax plan of Senator Bill Bradley (Democrat of New

---

5. U.S. Department of the Treasury, *Tax Reform for Fairness, Simplicity, and Economic Growth: The Treasury Department Report to the President*, 3 vols. (Treasury Department, 1984).

Jersey) and Representative Richard A. Gephardt (Democrat of Missouri);[6] and the "FAST" tax plan of Representative Jack Kemp (Republican of New York) and Senator Bob Kasten (Republican of Wisconsin).[7] All three would reduce or terminate most nonrevenue uses of the tax system by scaling back or eliminating most special deductions, credits, and exclusions for both individuals and businesses. We conclude that the Treasury plan is the most promising of the three because it not only broadens the tax base and reduces tax rates but, unlike the other two, also reduces inflation-related distortions and moves toward a more efficient system of taxing corporations. The Bradley-Gephardt proposal also would represent an enormous improvement over the current tax system. The Kemp-Kasten proposal contains important reforms as well but suffers from significant, although correctable, flaws.

However, none of the three plans deals adequately with the distortions of saving under current law, the bias toward activities on which tax liabilities can be deferred, and (despite the progress shown in the Treasury proposal) the extra tax burdens placed on activities carried out by corporations. To correct these problems would require more far-reaching changes than even these three proposals contemplate.

The Cash Flow Income Tax

Chapter 4 presents a plan that addresses all of the tax problems described in chapter 2. The plan is a "cash flow" income tax, under which individuals would pay tax on all cash receipts, less deductions for saving. Savings would eventually be taxed when they are used to finance consumption or when they are transferred to other people by gift or bequest. The taxation of gifts and bequests distinguishes the cash flow income tax from so-called consumed income taxes, which tax only consumption and not wealth transferred from generation to generation. Corporations would also be subject to a cash flow income tax, which would fall on all cash distributions to shareholders.

In some respects, the cash flow income tax resembles the plans examined in chapter 3. For example, it would repeal most special deductions, credits, and exclusions and reduce marginal tax rates. Like the Treasury plan, the cash flow income tax would end the distortions in

6. S. 409, H.R. 800.
7. S. 325, H.R. 777.

the taxation of capital income caused by inflation, although the mechanism for correcting these distortions would be more precise than it is under the Treasury plan.

Unlike the plans examined in chapter 3, however, the cash flow income tax would also remove the favoritism in current law shown toward activities on which taxes can be deferred; it would end the bias toward immediate consumption of income; and it would integrate corporation and personal income taxes. An appendix to chapter 4 examines important practical problems in applying the cash flow income tax: how to tax borrowing, owner-occupied housing, capital gains on consumption goods, outlays on education and training, and trusts; and how to treat migration, multinational businesses, and state income taxes.

Sales Taxes

As a device for raising revenue, sales taxes can be extremely effective. A practical tax on consumer goods and services would raise about $17 billion per percentage point of tax in 1986. Many advocates of greater reliance on sales taxes have also argued that such taxes would increase household saving. Chapter 5 examines the two major approaches to the taxation of consumer goods and services—a value-added tax and a national sales tax. Although they would cover most types of consumption, these taxes would exempt a sizable fraction of consumption outlays—perhaps 50 percent or more—in an effort to lighten tax burdens on the poor or to simplify administration. Chapter 5 also describes a number of possible taxes on energy, including taxes on imported petroleum, all petroleum and related products, and all energy. In addition to raising considerable revenue, such taxes would discourage energy consumption and some would encourage domestic exploration.

We conclude that these sales taxes, despite their revenue-raising potential, are all seriously flawed, for the following reasons. First, although they would reduce the need to increase income tax rates, none would do anything to remove the serious distortions of the personal and corporation income taxes. Second, they would add significantly to the taxes of those now regarded as too poor to pay income taxes. Third, the methods that could offset these burdens on the poor would come at the cost of substantial complexity for taxpayers and tax administrators. Fourth, general sales taxes or value-added taxes would represent federal encroachment on fiscal territory previously reserved for states and localities. Fifth, the introduction of these taxes would likely trigger a period of increased inflation. Last, international experience suggests that alleged advantages of sales taxes—the encouragement of saving and assistance to international trade—have been greatly exaggerated. One is left with the conclusion that sales taxes are effective instruments for raising taxes but not for reforming them.

Chapter 5 also describes a type of value-added tax designed by Robert Hall and Alvin Rabushka. The Hall-Rabushka plan is superior to conventional value-added taxes because it exempts persons with low earnings. Moreover, the Hall-Rabushka plan, unlike other sales tax proposals, is intended not merely to raise revenue but to replace the existing personal and corporation income tax structure. We conclude chapter 5 by showing how to preserve certain administrative advantages of the Hall-Rabushka plan while bringing the base closer to that of an annual income tax or a cash flow income tax.

Short-Term Measures to Cut the Deficit

However strong the case for reform may be, far-reaching legislation will take time to enact and to implement. Because large budget deficits threaten to damage the economy, we examine in chapter 6 a number of "quick fixes"—simple plans that raise some of the revenue needed to close the deficit and that may achieve some modest improvements in tax structure. Two of these approaches would increase taxes across the board. The first is a temporary increase in tax rates; the second is an expansion of the tax base. An example of the latter approach is disallowance of a flat percentage of currently permitted deductions, credits, and exclusions as proposed by Representative Fortney H. (Pete) Stark (Democrat of California) and Senator John H. Chafee (Republican of Rhode Island). On economic grounds, we favor base broadening, because this approach increases tax burdens most for those who most aggressively use special provisions to avoid taxes. In addition, base broadening at least points in the direction of structural reform by reducing distortions in the tax base, whereas rate increases add to them.

The critical question about short-run plans, however, does not concern the progress that they make toward tax reform; none goes very far. The more important question about temporary plans concerns their prospects for gaining prompt acceptance. These prospects are also addressed in chapter 6.

Political Strategies to Achieve Reform

No matter how good or bad a comprehensive tax reform plan may be, it will succeed or fail in the political arena. The political history of tax reform is, to put the matter gently, not encouraging; chapter 7 explains why this is so and suggests a strategy for doing better in the future.

Tax reform is politically difficult in large part because particular groups of taxpayers that stand to lose a lot from tax changes are willing to spend a lot to prevent them. In an effort to influence congressional votes, those opposed to change may take a range of actions—from straightforward information campaigns to promises or threats regarding campaign contributions. The districts of members of Congress are likely to contain disproportionate numbers of the beneficiaries of one special tax provision or another. Acting purely as public-spirited representatives of their constituents, good politicians can be expected to defend provisions of particular local benefit, although the national interest may not be served.

Given the strong forces resisting change, successful tax reform is impossible to imagine without powerful leadership from the president. Only the president represents the national constituency. For tax reform to succeed, a popular president must adopt it as a major initiative and be willing to call in political debts to secure its passage. In addition, Congress must fashion internal procedures to minimize opportunities for individual representatives or senators to secure "just this one exception for just this one worthy cause." The accumulation of such exceptions is one of the most important reasons for the sad state of the tax system.

Chapter 7 concludes that the political conditions for far-reaching and successful tax reform are hard but not impossible to create. Above all, the nation must appreciate the extreme importance of tax reform so that the effort to bring it about can be rightly regarded as a patriotic and statesmanlike act. A just and efficient tax system is fundamental to the effective operation of a democratic society. The tax system can hobble the economy, or it can encourage economic growth. It can bog down taxpayers in trying to avoid taxes and in trying to find their ways through legal mazes, or it can leave individuals free to pursue activities of benefit both to themselves and to society. It can undermine allegiance by spreading the suspicion that at tax-paying time one must either cheat or be cheated, or it can sustain each citizen's faith that all share fairly in the costs of maintaining a free nation.

CHAPTER TWO

Thinking about Tax Reform

THINKING SENSIBLY about tax reform requires that one have in mind an ideal tax system against which proposals can be evaluated. Without such an ideal, one cannot decide whether any proposed change is an improvement. Unfortunately, people disagree strenuously about what the ideal tax system should look like. Many think that the tax system should be used to influence private economic and social choices. Many others hold, as we do, that frequent use of the tax system to change private incentives will lead to inequity and unintended distortions.

Disagreements on the nature of the ideal tax system extend beyond the question of the system's purpose. They also encompass the most fundamental issue for levying taxes: what is the best way to measure an individual's ability to pay? Some hold that annual income (measured as the sum of consumption plus additions to net worth over the year) best measures ability to pay taxes. Others claim that income measured over many years or that annual consumption expenditures are better measures.

This chapter examines many of the issues about which tax reformers disagree and provides necessary background for evaluating the various plans detailed in chapters 3, 4, and 5. We warn readers that this chapter may not be easy going despite our best efforts to be clear and straightforward. But the issues raised here are important. It is impossible to think straight about tax policy options without a thorough understanding of the objectives sought in a desirable system.

The chapter is divided into four parts. The first concerns whether taxes should be used not only to collect enough money to pay for public expenditures but also to promote social and economic objectives. The second and third parts examine the concepts of fairness and economic efficiency, respectively, and the principles of taxation that emerge from them. The fourth part covers enforcement and compliance and the problems of transition following tax reform.

Nonrevenue Objectives of Taxation

The dateline on the news story was Washington, D.C. The text was as follows:

Most members of both houses of Congress today embraced a new homeownership assistance program. Under this program homeowners will be entitled to rebates based on the amount of their mortgages and the interest rate on those mortgages.

Unlike many assistance programs, however, the amount of aid will rise with income, and there will be no limit on the maximum payment. Four-person families with incomes of less than $7,400 will be entirely ineligible for aid. So will any family whose housing payments for mortgage interest plus certain other payments are less than $3,400.

The payments will begin at as little as 11 percent of qualifying expenditures by single persons with incomes of less than $3,400, and four-person families with incomes of less than $7,400. The maximum subsidy of 50 percent of qualifying expenditures will be available only to single persons with incomes of more than $85,800 and to four-person families with incomes of more than $166,400.

The new program will be administered in a novel way. Instead of processing applications for assistance, the government will pay funds automatically to anyone who fills out a simple form. The government intends to audit only about 2 percent of all such forms for accuracy and honesty. "It sure keeps down the size of the bureaucracy," one skeptical critic quipped.

When asked whether it was true that some upper income families might receive $10,000 per year or more under the program, while some lower income families receive nothing, the bill's sponsors acknowledged that such an outcome was anticipated. Despite a study by the Congressional Budget Office showing that more than half of the subsidies under this homeownership-promotion program would accrue to households with incomes of $50,000 per year or more and virtually none to households with incomes of $10,000 per year or less, no one in Congress, the current administration, or in any previous administration could be found to criticize the plan on the record.

The foregoing news report is fictional. No one has ever sponsored such a ridiculous expenditure program, one that in the name of promoting homeownership would give vast sums to households that can easily afford costly homes while denying any aid to those for whom even modest housing outlays are burdensome.

Or so one might think. In fact, Congress supports a "homeownership assistance" program that has exactly the same effects as the absurd expenditure program just described. It is the deduction for mortgage interest under the personal income tax. Far from criticizing it, most members of Congress regard it as politically sacrosanct.

The mortgage interest deduction illustrates the key pitfall of promoting social and economic objectives through the tax system. Inefficient and inequitable patterns of assistance, which would be obvious in a direct expenditure program, are camouflaged when provided indirectly through the tax system.[1] The exclusion of fringe benefits and transfer payments, the charitable deduction, the extra exemption for the aged and blind, the deduction for interest on consumer durables, the deductions for spending on various investment goods, and virtually all other special personal and business exclusions and deductions (other than ordinary business expenses) provide the greatest assistance to people and businesses in the highest tax brackets and none at all to people who use the standard deduction or who, for other reasons, have no taxable income.

Tax subsidies generally escape the scrutiny that automatically falls on expenditure programs. Had they been presented as expenditures, virtually none of the deductions just listed could have survived the devastating criticisms they would certainly have encountered. Once enshrined in the tax code, however, they are hard to remove for several reasons. First, although the pattern of assistance may be bizarre, most of these provisions promote activities that Congress and the American people genuinely want to encourage, such as homeownership, charitable giving, health insurance, pollution abatement, and energy conservation. Most of these tax provisions, though poorly designed and inefficient, advance their stated objectives in some degree. If they were repealed, Congress would have to decide whether it wished to implement other, better-designed measures to promote those objectives.

Second, many people have made investments on the assumption that these provisions will continue. The abrupt repeal of the mortgage interest deduction, for example, would sharply reduce the after-tax incomes of many families whose home purchases were based on the continued existence of the deduction, and it would probably cause the prices of owner-occupied housing to fall.

Third, assistance provided through the tax code is advantageous to beneficiaries precisely because it receives less searching scrutiny before and after enactment than do direct expenditures. Few tax provisions are

1. Stanley S. Surrey, *Pathways to Tax Reform: The Concept of Tax Expenditures* (Harvard University Press, 1973).

drafted to expire at specific dates. None requires an explicit appropriation. Furthermore, beneficiaries rarely view themselves as objects of largesse when they take a deduction, calculate a credit, or perform some other tax-reducing computation on their tax forms. For these reasons, assistance provided through the tax system is in less political jeopardy than that provided through direct expenditures. And no one knows that better than the beneficiaries themselves.

Finally, tax provisions, in contrast to direct expenditures or government regulations, seem to promote desired objectives without increasing government employment or the budget. This perception has a deceptive element of reality. The deduction for mortgage interest does indeed take fewer federal officials to administer and adds less to government spending than would direct grants to would-be homeowners. But the administrative savings result entirely because standards of enforcement that would be considered scandalous in a spending program are readily accepted for tax provisions. If the same standards of screening and verification were required of people who apply for federal assistance of other kinds, administrative costs would be much the same.

Furthermore, each tax provision adds just as much to the federal deficit as would equally costly direct grants. The budgetary cost of encouraging homeownership through the tax system is much higher, in fact, if one recognizes that most of the tax savings go to people who would buy a home even without them. Any savings in federal employment result from stinting on oversight and accepting a scattershot distribution of benefits that would be intolerable in a spending program.

The foregoing criticism of tax provisions designed to achieve nonrevenue objectives does not denigrate the objectives themselves, many of which are meritorious. We do not claim that tax provisions should never be used for nonrevenue objectives; in fact, we make a few such proposals in chapter 4. Nor do we claim that revenues generated by the repeal of special deductions, exclusions, or credits necessarily should be retained in the public sector; instead, they could be used to cut marginal tax rates along the lines proposed in chapters 3 or 4. Alternatively, the revenues could pay for expenditures to promote the same goals the tax provisions so inefficiently advance. Or they could be used to help solve the deficit problem described in chapter 1. The choice would be up to Congress.

We share the view that repeal of most special deductions, credits, and allowances would be a significant step forward. But a reduction in the number and dollar cost of these provisions is not the only, or even the major, issue in tax reform. Such changes would represent only the first steps necessary to make the tax system fairer, more conducive to economic growth and efficiency, and more easily administered.

Fairness

Fairness is the equal treatment of persons in equal circumstances. If this condition is violated, people will be treated inequitably, and incentives will be created to base economic decisions on tax considerations rather than on true economic gain. The critical issue is how to determine when people are in equal economic circumstances. We divide the issue of fairness into the following questions. What flows best measure ability to pay? Over what period should these flows be measured and taxed? Should taxes be levied only on actual transactions or also on accruals, that is, on unrealized changes in asset values? How should the distorting effects of inflation be handled? And last, what system of taxation minimizes distortions in saving?

Ability to Pay

Fairness dictates that those with the same ability to pay should pay the same tax. But according to what measure can it be said that taxpayer A has the same ability to pay as taxpayer B? This question has been hotly debated for centuries and is not resolved in the current income tax system. The debate ranges over two dimensions: the object to be measured—income or consumption—and the period over which the object should be measured—the so-called accounting period.

INCOME VERSUS CONSUMPTION. Some economists and philosophers have held that consumption, not income, should be the base for direct personal taxation.[2] They have held that justice requires taxes to be apportioned on the basis of what people withdraw from the pool of resources (consumption) instead of what they contribute to it (earnings plus the return to savings). They have argued that consumption can be measured far more reliably and simply than income. And they have held

2. Thomas Hobbes, *Leviathan* (Macmillan, 1962); Nicholas Kaldor, *An Expenditure Tax* (London: Allen and Unwin, 1955); Irving Fisher, "Income in Theory and Income Taxation in Practice," *Econometrica*, vol. 5 (January 1937), pp. 1–55.

that consumption is a more stable tax base because household consumption varies less than household income.

Each of these propositions is debatable, but consumption in our view is simply not an accurate measure of each person's ability to pay or of total economic capacity. Accumulations of wealth confer valuable economic and social benefits to their owners even if the wealth is not consumed. Accordingly, wealth accumulations should be incorporated into any measure of ability to pay. Unlike a consumption tax, a tax on income can reach accumulations of wealth that are not actually consumed during the accounting period. Thus we take income to be the proper object by which to measure ability to pay.

Having chosen income as the object of taxation, one must devise rules for measuring it. Income can be measured in two ways: as an inflow and as an outflow. As an inflow, income equals the sum of earnings plus returns to capital, including changes in the value of assets. As an outflow, income equals the sum of consumption plus additions to net worth. These two definitions are equivalent to each other—dollars coming in equal dollars going out or retained. The number of dollars in the tax base is the same in either case.

THE ACCOUNTING PERIOD. Income can be measured and taxed over a day, a week, a month, a year, or a period as long as the taxpayer's life.[3] The U.S. income tax uses an annual taxation period,[4] the same as that recommended by Henry Simons and Robert Murray Haig, two professors whose writings on taxation undergird much academic analysis of the income tax.[5] Fundamentally, however, there is no logical reason

3. If one believes that people care as much about their heirs' ability to consume as about their own, then the appropriate equity comparison is not between two individuals over their lifetimes but between two multigenerational families extending indefinitely into the future. Equity would then require that two such dynastic families with equal resources be taxed the same. This approach implies a pure consumption tax, because a tax on consumption plus accumulations of wealth not consumed but transferred to one's heirs would reduce the consumption opportunities of subsequent generations by a greater proportion than it reduces the consumption opportunities of the current generation. However, aside from the obvious problem of defining the dynastic tax unit, we find it hard to accept that the basic principle of tax equity should be the equal taxation of intergenerational dynasties with equal resources.

4. In certain highly restricted circumstances individuals may average income over four to ten years.

5. Henry Simons, *Personal Income Taxation: The Definition of Income as a Problem of Fiscal Policy* (University of Chicago Press, 1938); Robert Murray Haig, "The Concept of Income: Economic and Legal Aspects," in Robert Murray Haig, ed., *The Federal Income Tax* (Columbia University Press, 1921).

why a particular astronomical regularity should be enshrined in the tax law.

To be sure, there may be practical as well as historical reasons for choosing one income definition and accounting period over the other. Inflows rather than outflows may better conform with conventional views as to what income really is. Similarly, there may be practical and historical reasons for treating equally individuals who have the same one-year income but not the same multiyear or lifetime income. We shall explore later the implications of choosing different accounting periods. This choice affects the equity, efficiency, and administration of the tax system in ways that are not initially obvious. For now, the main point is that one can favor income over consumption as the measure of ability to pay without necessarily favoring a single year as the best accounting period for determining equally situated taxpayers.

Accrual or Realization

The income tax rests on the concept that annual income, when measured as an inflow, includes changes in the value of assets. For practical reasons, however, most personal income is not taxed when it accrues to the benefits of the taxpayer but only when it is realized, generally in a market transaction. This conflict between the definition of income in concept and its measurement in practice is responsible for much inequity, inefficiency, and complexity in the current tax law. For example, capital gains and losses on assets such as closely held corporations, works of art and jewelry, and any other asset for which no objective market price is available can only be estimated crudely and laboriously. Gains and losses on assets such as stocks traded on registered exchanges are easily counted and could be easily taxed when they accrue. But taxing some assets one way and some another would create unfair distinctions among assets and among taxpayers. Instead, current law taxes only realized capital gains, thus abandoning the principle that annual economic income should be taxed. As a result, a different set of unfair distinctions is created: taxpayers with accrued but unrealized capital gains pay significantly less tax than do others with realized gains, although their economic incomes are identical.

Why should capital gains be taxed the same whether or not they are realized? Because it is not necessary to realize a capital gain in order to spend it. If one pledges the appreciated asset as security on a loan, one can spend the proceeds of the loan and even deduct the interest payments on the loan, thus reducing current tax liabilities. As long as the asset continues to appreciate by an amount at least equal to the after-tax interest cost, one can quite literally have one's wine and drink it too.[6]

The preferred treatment accorded to capital gains is pervasive. Gains on almost all capital assets are not taxed until realized, and only 40 percent of long-term gains are included in taxable income.[7] Perhaps most important is the fact that most capital gains are not realized and are never subject to income tax.[8] Gains transferred to others by gift or bequest are not taxable to the donor, and, in the case of bequests, the basis used in calculating any tax on heirs is the value of the asset at time of inheritance. Thus, appreciation during the life of the donor forever escapes tax.

The result of these inconsistent rules is that people whose economic incomes are identical may pay very different amounts of tax. Consider three people in the 50 percent tax bracket, each of whom holds two assets. One asset was purchased for $1,000 and one for $7,000; both are now worth $4,000. Both assets have been held at least six months, which means 40 percent of realized gains on them are taxable.[9] One person sells only the appreciated asset and therefore owes $600 in taxes on the transaction (50 percent tax on 40 percent of the $3,000 gain). A second person sells only the depreciated asset and, because the loss is deducted from taxable income, saves $600 in taxes (50 percent tax on 40 percent of the $3,000 loss). The third person sells both assets (or neither of them) and experiences no tax liability and no tax saving. Yet all three people

6. The ability to realize losses, retain gains, and deduct interest expense currently, plus the difference between tax rates on long- and short-term capital gains and the availability of "hedging" devices in financial transactions enable investors to reduce, if not to eliminate, tax on all income. The technically inclined reader is referred to Joseph E. Stiglitz, "Some Aspects of the Taxation of Capital Gains," *Journal of Public Economics*, vol. 21 (July 1983), pp. 257–94.

7. One exception is capital gains earned in the rapidly growing markets in futures contracts. All futures contracts are treated as if they were realized at year-end, and 64 percent of net gains or net losses are used in computing taxable income. This and all subsequent discussions of specific provisions of current law refer to the Internal Revenue Code of 1954, as amended.

8. See Martin J. Bailey, "Capital Gains and Income Taxation," in Martin J. Bailey and Arnold C. Harberger, eds., *The Taxation of Income from Capital* (Brookings, 1969), pp. 11–49.

9. The qualitative relationship among the tax liabilities of the three people is exactly the same if the asset has been held less than six months. The tax consequences would be two and one-half times greater.

have the same income (change in net worth) from their assets; and each person who sells just one asset realizes the same amount of cash.[10]

The tension between realizations and accruals contributes to the horrendous complexity of the tax system. For example, particularly abstruse provisions in the code have been added to prevent taxpayers from borrowing money, deducting the interest expenses, and escaping current tax on appreciating assets bought with the borrowed funds. Specifically, deductions of interest expenses incurred to acquire investment property, categorized as "investment interest" expense, are limited to the sum of net investment income plus $10,000, and only those who itemize their personal deductions may deduct such interest. These interest expenses are distinguished from interest incurred by a trade or business, which is always deductible, and from other interest expenses, such as mortgage and consumer installment interest, which are deductible in full but only by those who itemize their deductions.

These distinctions prevent only blatant and clumsy abuses. In most cases, however, people can avoid the restrictions by restructuring their borrowing. These provisions also discriminate against borrowers whose only collateral is investment property and in favor of those who can either liquidate assets, preferably those with losses, or can borrow in a form such that the interest deductions are unrestricted. Thus, a person who can remortgage a home, borrow against a business, or sell other interest-bearing assets will not be materially affected by limitations on the deductibility of interest. In contrast, these provisions can place people with little wealth at a serious disadvantage. Those with few assets or little capital income usually have few opportunities for such tax gamesmanship. These examples illustrate the tendency of the tax system to give more help to those who already possess substantial wealth than to those seeking to acquire it.[11]

10. In some cases, people enjoy increases in net worth but not in their current capacity to spend or to pay taxes. A person who accrues rights to pensions payable in the future assuredly has enjoyed an increase in net worth but may not have experienced any increase in current spending capacity, because it is not permissible, in general, to pledge entitlements to future pension payments as security for loans. If an annual income tax based consistently on accrual principles were to be implemented in circumstances where such liquidity problems were severe, special arrangements for the calculation and future payment of taxes would be required.

11. See Eugene Steuerle, "Building New Wealth by Preserving Old Wealth: Savings and Investment Tax Incentives in the Postwar Era," *National Tax Journal,* vol. 36 (September 1983), pp. 307–19.

Inflation

Proper measurement of income requires the valuation of all quantities in real terms, that is, with full adjustments for inflation. If such adjustments are not made, inflation changes both the tax base and tax rates.

A simple example shows how inflation distorts the tax base. A person who sells corporate stock at a profit will pay taxes on the difference between the purchase price and the selling price. If the general price level rose faster than the price of the stock, so that the proceeds from the sale buy less than did the funds used to acquire the stock, the same tax would still be due. In this situation, taxable income has little or no relation to economic income, and taxpayers in the same real economic circumstances may pay widely different taxes; thus the interaction of the tax system with inflation undermines equity. The serious misallocation of resources that these distortions can cause are discussed in more detail below in the section on efficiency and growth.

Inflation also pushes taxpayers into progressively higher tax brackets. Discretionary tax reductions more than offset "bracket creep" for most taxpayers from 1960 through the mid-1970s. From 1978 until 1985, however, Congress made no adjustments in personal exemptions or the standard deduction (zero-bracket amount). As a result, households with incomes below the poverty thresholds, who had been largely exempt from personal income taxes, increasingly became subject to them. In the Economic Recovery Tax Act of 1981 Congress solved this problem by providing automatic adjustments of personal exemptions, bracket widths, and the zero-bracket amount to offset the effects of inflation.

Saving Versus Consumption

It is generally regarded as unfair to tax people more heavily because they prefer oranges to apples, unless eating oranges is harmful or eating apples is particularly beneficial. If equals should be taxed equally, a preference for one kind of fruit over another should not affect tax liabilities. In the same sense, two people with the same consumption opportunities should not bear different tax burdens because one wants to consume apples or any other consumer goods immediately and the other wishes to save now and consume these goods in the future.

The annual taxation of capital incomes, even when executed consistently, violates the principle of fairness by discouraging future consump-

Table 2-1. *Effects of Annual Income Tax and Tax on Consumption Opportunities*
Percent

Tax	Earnings consumed immediately		Earnings saved at annual rate of 12 percent for consumption after thirty-five years	
	Consumption (dollars)	Reduction in consumption because of tax (percent)	Consumption (dollars)	Reduction in consumption because of tax (percent)
No tax	1,000	0	52,810	0
Annual income tax of 50 percent	500	50	3,843	93
Tax of 50 percent on consumption opportunities	500	50	26,405	50

tion. The following example illustrates the problem. Two people each have $1,000 of income. They can consume the income now or invest it and earn 12 percent per year. One person consumes $1,000 immediately. The other uses the $1,000 to buy an asset yielding 12 percent per year and holds it for thirty-five years; at that point the saver would have $52,810 in the absence of taxes (see table 2-1). If a 50 percent annual income tax is imposed, both people will pay half of the $1,000 income in the current year and the saver will pay half of the 12 percent annual return as it accrues. The person who consumes immediately pays half the $1,000 income in taxes and will have half to consume, a 50 percent reduction in consumption possibilities. The person who saves will pay $48,967 in taxes and will be able to consume only $3,843 after thirty-five years, a 93 percent reduction in consumption possibilities. The large extra burden on the person who chooses to postpone consumption arises because the tax not only falls on the $1,000 earned but also reduces the net rate of return from 12 percent to 6 percent.[12] There is no good reason why the exercise of a choice available to both should result in such

12. In the absence of taxes, a person could save $1,000; at 12 percent compound interest, this sum would accumulate to $52,810 after thirty-five years. After paying 50 percent tax, the saver would have $26,405 to spend. Under a 50 percent annual income tax, the person retains $500 after tax and can earn only 6 percent on savings after payment of taxes. After thirty-five years, $500 grows at 6 percent compound interst to $3,843, a sum that is only 7 percent of the tax-free accumulation. The reduction in consumption opportunities in the first case is 50 percent and in the second 93 percent ($3,843 / $52,810 = 0.07) .

grossly unequal tax rates. Yet no other outcome is possible if the requirements of an annual income tax are rigorously observed.

CURRENT LAW. The current U.S. tax system does not follow all requirements of annual income taxation. Instead, uneasy compromises are made in the treatment of saving. In some cases, capital income is taxed annually whether or not consumed; in other cases, tax-induced inequities are avoided through the use of a multiyear or lifetime accounting period. For example, deposits and interest earnings of qualified pension plans and other individual retirement accounts are untaxed until they are withdrawn, typically many years later. Because the return to saving is not taxed until withdrawal, often for retirement consumption, those choosing future consumption rather than current consumption are not differentially taxed, thus avoiding the inequity faced by the person in the above example who chose to save.

ALTERNATIVE APPROACHES. The goal of taxing equally those who wish to consume now and those who wish to use their income later can be reached in either of two ways. The first entails a tax whenever consumption occurs. If such a tax were imposed at the rate of 50 percent, the person in the example presented above who chooses current consumption would pay a $500 tax and be able to spend $500, as shown in the third row of table 2-1. If the income is saved and consumption is postponed for thirty-five years, consumption would then equal $26,405, half of the pre-tax amount. Such a tax would not discriminate among taxpayers on the basis of when they wished to use their income. Both current consumers and future consumers would find their opportunities to spend reduced by 50 percent.

Penalties on those who choose to postpone consumption can be avoided in another way. Tax could be levied on receipts of wages and salaries, but all returns from saving would be exempt. Under certain conditions, those with the same initial earnings and different preferences for saving would be taxed equally under either of the two approaches.[13]

If, however, bequests, gifts, and inheritances are not included in the tax system, the two tax approaches—taxing earnings or taxing consumption—are no longer equivalent because some sources or some uses of income would be disregarded. More important, the two approaches would not conform to basic principles of equity. If only earnings were taxed, it would be possible for people with large inheritances to consume

13. See, for example, Anthony B. Atkinson and Joseph E. Stiglitz, *Lectures on Public Economics* (McGraw-Hill, 1980), pp. 69–70.

out of their inherited wealth without incurring any tax liability in their lifetime. If the tax were based only on consumption, it would be possible for people to avoid tax by making bequests or gifts to others. The failure to include gifts and bequests in the tax base of both donors and beneficiaries is inconsistent with the principle that tax burdens should be a function of each person's full ability to pay.[14]

Inheritances, bequests, and gifts can be handled in either of two ways. Tax could be imposed on all earnings plus inheritances and gifts received, an "opportunities" approach that would tax initial opportunities or expected returns from saving, not actual outcomes. People with equal earnings who saved equal amounts but who earned varying rates on their savings would all pay the same tax and end with widely different disposable incomes, because returns on investments would go untaxed.

Alternatively, tax could be based on "outcomes"—consumption plus gifts and bequests—not on initial opportunities. This approach would impose equal taxes on two people with different earnings who saved different amounts but whose rates of return just compensated for these differentials.[15] If people make investments that have uncertain outcomes, they can achieve the same results under the opportunities approach as under the outcomes approach, provided that they can invest as much or as little as they wish.[16]

---

14. It may be useful to note that the Treasury Department report, *Blueprints for Basic Tax Reform,* contrasted an ability-to-pay measure of the tax base (in which transfers given are included in the tax base of the donor) from a standard-of-living measure (in which such transfers are not included). See also the discussion of this issue in the revised version, David F. Bradford and the U.S. Treasury Department Tax Policy Staff, *Blueprints for Basic Tax Reform,* 2d ed. (Arlington, Va.: Tax Analysts, 1984), pp. xvi–xvii.

15. For example, person A earns $1,000 and saves it all, and the principle doubles to $2,000; person B earns $500 and saves it all, and the principle quadruples to $2,000. Persons A and B each would pay the same tax upon consumption of $2,000.

16. For example, if the tax rate is 50 percent, it makes no difference to the investor whether a deduction is allowed for a $2,000 investment, in which case the net cost is $1,000, and taxes are paid on the proceeds from the investment, or whether no deduction is allowed for a $1,000 investment, and no taxes are paid on the proceeds. In both cases, the person has invested $1,000 of personal resources and receives an after-tax rate of return on that investment equal to the before-tax rate of return. More generally, if t is the tax rate, a person who invests K and is taxed on the opportunities basis is in the same position as an investor who is taxed on an outcomes basis and invests $K \times [1/(1 - t)]$. The equivalency of the opportunities and outcomes approaches breaks down when investment opportunities are constrained by external circumstances. It is unlikely, for example, that the entrepreneurs who began Polaroid Corp., Xerox Corp.,

The opportunities approach includes in the recipient's tax base inheritances and gifts received but allows the donor no deductions for gifts and bequests made. Under the outcomes approach, the donor pays tax on gifts and bequests, and the recipient is allowed no deductions for outlays on consumption, gifts, or bequests financed from inherited wealth.

Whichever approach is taken, a tax of x percent causes after-tax resources to be exactly x percent below what they would be if no tax were imposed. Because actual realized rates of return differ enormously, we believe that the outcomes approach would generally be perceived as much fairer, although in many cases the difference between the two approaches is only apparent, not real. Under the outcomes approach, two taxpayers would be considered to be in equal circumstances if they have used the same quantity of resources for consumption, gifts, and bequests over their lifetimes. In terms of the accounting identity presented in the section above on ability to pay, these rules result in a tax on income measured by all uses of resources instead of all receipts.[17] The resulting tax is different from a consumption tax, which would fall only on consumption and which would exclude changes in net worth by exempting gifts and bequests.

Efficiency and Growth

Almost all taxes distort economic decisions.[18] Some distortions arise from explicit efforts by Congress to influence economic and social

---

or MCI Communications Corp. had much opportunity to calibrate their investments in the way an investor in widely traded securities might do.

17. Economists should recognize that this method of measuring income is simply the familiar Haig-Simons definition of income extended from one year to the lifetime and expressed in present-value terms. Because of its similarity to the *annual* Haig-Simons income tax, one might refer to this tax as a *lifetime* income tax, because it would impose tax on total consumption plus change in net worth summed over an individual's lifetime. See Richard A. Musgrave, "ET, OT, and SBT," *Journal of Public Economics*, vol. 16 (July–August 1976), pp. 3–16; and "The Nature of Horizontal Equity and the Principle of Broad-Based Taxation: A Friendly Critique," in John G. Head, ed., *Taxation Issues of the 1980s* (Melbourne: Australian Tax Research Foundation, 1983), pp. 21–33. For measures of the effects of excluding bequests from such a tax base, see Paul L. Menchik and Martin David, "The Incidence of a Lifetime Consumption Tax," *National Tax Journal*, vol. 35 (June 1982), pp. 189–203.

18. About the only exceptions are lump sum poll taxes, but they are generally regarded as unfair and are seldom used. Even poll taxes may influence migration, and for this reason may not be entirely free of distortionary effects.

behavior. At the beginning of this chapter we examined the pros and cons of using the tax system to achieve special social and economic objectives. With few exceptions, the resulting tax provisions are inefficient instruments for achieving these goals. They make compliance and enforcement difficult, and they encourage taxpayers to undertake complex transactions to avoid taxes. The most important distortions, however, arise because basic tax rules, those intended only to raise revenue and not to promote or discourage particular actions, produce incentives that their authors did not anticipate. Like the planned incentives intended for special purposes, these unplanned incentives increase complexity and unfairness and usually reduce economic efficiency.

Market economies are based on the principle that most transactions undertaken voluntarily by individuals and businesses cannot be improved by external management. If the decisions made in the absence of taxes would have been economically efficient, tax-induced changes in those decisions can only make things worse. Although there are important exceptions to this principle,[19] few of the unintended distortions arising from the present tax system can be justified on the ground that they offset natural inefficiencies. The large distortions of investment decisions that arise from variations in effective tax rates have no consistent rationale.[20] In addition, the highly uneven treatment of savings and asset income cannot be explained by market imperfections that the tax system is designed to correct.

19. When the actions of one person or business affect others and no market exists to take these effects into account, or when buyers and sellers lack important information and cannot obtain it, taxes may correct market-generated inefficiencies. For example, it may improve efficiency to tax goods that produce harmful byproducts.

20. Tax-induced distortions may not reduce overall efficiency if other distortions exist in the economy. In this event, the tax-induced distortions may offset the other distortions. Once distortions exist, some nonuniform pattern of tax rates generally is necessary to minimize total efficiency losses. However valid this point may be conceptually, no one knows what pattern of nonuniform tax rates would be optimal. There is no evidence that the current pattern of tax rates minimizes distortions. Given the enormous disparities in effective tax rates across activities, we believe that movement toward greater uniformity is highly likely to improve economic efficiency. For an excellent discussion of the sources of variations in effective tax rates, see Mervyn A. King and Don Fullerton, eds., *The Taxation of Income from Capital: A Comparative Study of the United States, the United Kingdom, Sweden, and West Germany* (University of Chicago Press, 1984). Also, see U.S. Department of the Treasury, *Tax Reform for Fairness, Simplicity, and Economic Growth: The Treasury Department Report to the President*, 3 vols., especially vol. 1: *Overview*, and vol. 2: *General Explanation of the Treasury Department Proposals* (Treasury Department, 1984).

Inflation

Among the most serious defects of the tax system are those that arise from its interaction with inflation. If a tax system is based on values unadjusted for inflation, it will mismeasure real economic depreciation, inventory costs, capital gains, and interest income and expense. This systematic mismeasurement of taxable income produces inequity, as we have already shown. But it also causes inefficiency by distorting economic decisions; and it adds to complexity by promoting transactions either to escape, or to capitalize on, the effects of inflation.

DEPRECIATION AND INVENTORY COSTS. Deductions for depreciation are based on historic costs if no adjustments are made for inflation. If depreciable lives reflect actual useful lives and prices are stable, depreciation deductions based on historic cost lead to an accurate measure of income; and if firms set the same amounts aside in depreciation reserves, they will build up a pool of funds sufficient to replace assets as they wear out. If prices increase, however, deductions fall short of replacement costs; the greater the rate of inflation, the greater the shortfall. In 1981 Congress tried to solve this problem by letting businesses take deductions for depreciation much faster than capital assets actually depreciate. Current law, for example, permits taxpayers to deduct the full cost of automobiles over three years, most equipment over five years, and most structures over eighteen years. Most of these items last far longer.

This acceleration of depreciation deductions exactly offsets the effects of inflation only at certain inflation rates: about 9½ percent for equipment of average life and about 15 percent for an average structure.[21] In general, the ratio of the present value of tax depreciation to real depreciation varies with both the rate of inflation and the durability of the asset. As a result, real effective tax rates on depreciable capital vary capriciously with inflation. Also, because of differences in the mix of assets used by various industries, changes in the rate of inflation alter relative tax

21. These calculations are based on lives of ten to twelve years for equipment and thirty-two years for structures. In fact, economic lives are estimated to range from five to twenty-five years for equipment and from sixteen to forty years for structures. The calculations used the methodology developed by Charles R. Hulten in "The Treasury Tax Proposal and the Prospects for Long-Run Growth" (Washington, D.C.: Urban Institute, January 1985). On the subject of true economic depreciation, see Charles R. Hulten and Frank C. Wykoff, "The Measurement of Economic Depreciation," in Charles R. Hulten, ed., *Depreciation, Inflation, and the Taxation of Income from Capital* (Washington, D.C.: Urban Institute, 1981), pp. 81–125.

Table 2-2. *Current Effective Tax Rates on Equity-Financed Investments in Equipment and Structures, by Industry and Inflation Rate, for a Taxpayer in the 46 Percent Bracket*
Percent

	Effective tax rate	
Industry	5% inflation	10% inflation
Agriculture	29	37
Mining	13	31
Logging	21	34
Wood products and furniture	28	38
Glass, cement, and clay	20	31
Primary metals	16	28
Fabricated metals	28	38
Machinery and instruments	26	36
Electrical equipment	26	38
Motor vehicles	8	26
Transportation equipment	25	36
Food	25	35
Tobacco	18	30
Textiles	19	32
Apparel	28	38
Pulp and paper	12	26
Printing and publishing	22	34
Chemicals	19	32
Petroleum refining	12	26
Rubber	18	30
Leather	30	40
Transport services	9	26
Utilities	28	38
Communications	19	33
Service and trade	31	40

Source: U.S. Department of the Treasury, *Tax Reform for Fairness, Simplicity, and Economic Growth: The Treasury Department Report to the President* (Treasury Department, 1984), p. 108.

burdens across industries (see table 2-2). Thus the reallocation of investment caused by the current system reflects no rational set of investment priorities. Basing depreciation deductions on true economic lives and adjusting historic costs for changes in the general price level since the asset was acquired would eliminate the variations in table 2-2.[22] Permitting businesses to deduct the full cost of investments immediately

22. Under an alternative approach suggested by Dale W. Jorgenson and Alan J. Auerbach, firms would receive an immediate deduction equal to the present value of the depreciation deductions to which they would be entitled if there were no inflation.

would also eliminate the variations, but in this case the deductibility of interest payments would have to be denied to prevent other distortions of investment decisions.[23]

Inflation and current tax laws also interact to distort inventory investment if goods remain in inventory for a significant amount of time. Most firms use the first-in-first-out (FIFO) method of calculating inventory costs. Under this rule, a firm's inventory accumulation, one element in the calculation of profits, is valued at the cost of the most recent acquisitions for inventory. In periods of inflation, this rule effectively allows the firm a deduction for items taken from inventory only at earlier acquisition costs, not at current prices, thereby overstating taxable income and tax liabilities.

Alternatively, firms can use the last-in-first-out (LIFO) method, which values inventories at earlier acquisition costs and as a result allows firms to deduct items taken from inventory as if they were the last purchased. If inventories are not decreasing, this procedure causes goods used in production to be valued at about their market cost. But it has two problems. First, because it places greater demands on record keeping, firms owning only about one-third of all inventories use it. Second, if a firm depletes its inventory, the value of the goods may be based on badly outdated prices. In this case, the allowable deduction for the cost of goods taken from inventory may greatly understate replacement cost and seriously overstate taxable profits. Thus when inventories are rising, LIFO protects firms against inflation, but when inventories are falling, LIFO is even worse than FIFO. The best procedure for offsetting the

---

This procedure avoids the need to make any explicit adjustments for inflation, because the deduction and the investment are made almost contemporaneously. It does, however, require estimates of the real interest rate to carry out the necessary discounting to present value and, for this reason, is not foolproof. See Alan J. Auerbach and Dale W. Jorgenson, "Inflation-proof Depreciation of Assets," *Harvard Business Review*, vol. 58 (September-October 1980), pp. 113–18.

23. Both the cash flow income tax discussed in chapter 4 and the Hall-Rabushka tax plan described in chapter 5 would allow expensing and would deny the interest deduction. For a demonstration that either true economic depreciation with interest deductibility or immediate expensing without interest deductibility causes no distortion of investment decisions, see Atkinson and Stiglitz, *Lectures on Public Finance*, pp. 145–49. The retention of interest deductibility with expensing is nondistorting if two conditions are satisfied. First, all borrowers and lenders must be in the same tax bracket, a condition unlikely to be satisfied except under a flat tax. Second, interest rates under deductibility (r') must be related to interest rates in the absence of deductibility (r) by the formula $r' = r/(1 + t)$, where t is the tax rate.

effect of inflation on inventory costs is to increase the deduction for goods taken from inventory by the change in the general price level between the time the good was bought and the time it was used.[24]

CAPITAL GAINS. Under current tax law capital gains are measured as the difference between the sales price of an asset and its "adjusted basis," the purchase price reduced by depreciation deductions allowed for depreciable assets. During inflation, however, the purchasing power of dollars received when an asset is sold is less than the purchasing power of dollars that were paid when the asset was purchased. Even modest inflation can create large distortions. At 5 percent annual inflation, prices double every fourteen years. That means that if a person holds an asset for fourteen years, during which prices rise 5 percent per year, assets must more than double in nominal (current) value before the owner enjoys any increase in real (that is, inflation-adjusted) net worth. At 10 percent inflation, prices double every seven years, and nominal asset prices would also have to double in that time before there was any real appreciation. Yet nominal gains are taxed even when there has been no real appreciation.

Current tax law deals with this problem only indirectly and crudely. The exclusion of 60 percent of gains on assets held longer than six months has been justified in part as a correction for inflation-related distortions, but is provides too little adjustment for gains from some asset sales, too much for others.[25]

The problem is aggravated, as noted in chapter 1, by the fact that taxpayers may buy assets with borrowed funds. Only 40 percent of long-term gains are subject to tax, but 100 percent of interest on loans is usually deductible; if interest rates are similar to the rate at which assets are appreciating, people can borrow to finance their purchases of such assets, deduct all of the interest, but pay tax on only 40 percent of the

24. See Henry J. Aaron, "Inflation and the Income Tax: An Introduction," in Henry J. Aaron, ed., *Inflation and the Income Tax* (Brookings, 1976), pp. 12–14.

25. Assume that an asset is purchased for $1,000 and is sold for $1,100 after ten years, during which time the general price level doubled. The nominal gain is $100. But there is a real loss of $900, because the inflation-corrected basis is $2,000—the original basis of $1,000, multiplied by the ratio of the price level in the year of sale to the price level in year of purchase. In this case, including only 40 percent of the nominal gain, or $40, corrects only a small part of the distortion. In contrast, if the asset was purchased for $50 and sold for $1,050 after a holding period during which prices doubled, exclusion of 60 percent of the nominal gain is too generous. In this case, the real gain is $950 (the $1,050 selling price less the inflation-corrected basis of $100); but only $400 of gain would be taxed.

gain. The potential for socially pointless tax avoidance is almost unlimited.

The proper way to calculate realized capital gains is to adjust the purchase price for inflation occurring between the date of purchase and the date of sale. If an asset were purchased for $1,000 and held for a period during which the general price level increased 50 percent, the taxable capital gain would be the excess of the selling price over $1,500. If the asset is sold for $2,000, the gain would be $500 (the $2,000 selling price less the inflation-corrected basis of $1,500). If the basis is corrected in this way, correct measurement of income requires the inclusion of the entire capital gain, regardless of the holding period.

INTEREST INCOME AND EXPENSE.   Inflation also causes mismeasurement of real interest income and expense. During inflation, interest payments compensate lenders not only for the use of their funds but also for the decline in the purchasing power of their funds over the life of the loan. The real income of the lender is the interest received (or accrued), less the decline in the real value of the loan principal outstanding. Similarly, the real interest expense of the borrower is the interest paid, less the fall in the real value of the outstanding loan.

Under current law, the interest on many loans is fully taxed, but the change in the value of the asset is ignored. For example, a person who pays $10,000 for a one-year asset yielding 10 percent, such as a one-year saving certificate or a one-year corporate bond, will receive $11,000 at year end: the $10,000 original principle plus $1,000 interest. If inflation is proceeding at 6 percent, the investor would have to end up with $10,600 just to retain the purchasing power held at the start of the year, that is, just to break even in real dollars. Hence, at 10 percent interest and 6 percent inflation, real income is $400. This investor should therefore have to report $400 in income, not $1,000 as under current law. Similarly, the borrower, who paid $1,000 in interest, should be permitted to deduct only $400 for real interest expense.

The implementation of this adjustment would be cumbersome. At the end of each tax period, taxpayers would have to measure the value of outstanding debt, multiply this sum by the rate of inflation, and subtract the product from nominal interest income and expense; only the difference would be used in calculating taxable income. For listed securities, the adjustment would be laborious, but for other securities, the task would be virtually insurmountable.[26] The practical question, therefore,

---

26. How, for example, would one value untraded risky bonds? How would one

is whether it is possible to reduce inflation-related distortions in interest income and expense in a practical way. The Treasury Department has proposed such an adjustment, which is described in chapter 3.

PROBLEMS OF INCOMPLETE INDEXATION.   If some but not all adjustments for inflation are made, inflation-related distortions can be reduced, but not all can be eliminated because combinations of transactions can be concocted to avoid taxes on real economic income. For example, if businesses are permitted to index their depreciation deductions but are not required to recognize inflation-related gains on debt, investments that readily lend themselves to debt finance will retain tax advantages over investments that do not. If businesses are required to adjust deductions for interest payments, but individuals are not, the tax law will continue to encourage borrowing by individuals.

Most economists agree that income tax rules must be altered to offset some of the effects of rapid inflation. Such adjustments might not remove every inflation-related opportunity for avoiding taxes, and they would add somewhat to the burden of compliance and administration. But they would simplify the lives of most taxpayers by discouraging transactions that are undertaken not for usual business purposes but purely because, during inflation, an unindexed system makes them so attractive.

There is no agreement on what rate of inflation justifies indexation.

---

adjust the implicit interest that arises in complex contracts when payments are scheduled at different times and may be contingent on future events? As unanticipated inflation causes market interest rates to rise, moreover, the value of a firm's outstanding debt declines. Is the inflation adjustment to be applied to this reduced market value of debt to calculate the firm's allowable interest deduction? In this event, changes in the value of the firm's outstanding debt resulting from factors quite unrelated to inflation, such as changes in the market's perception of the riskiness of the firm, would also affect the amount of the firm's interest deduction. Interest deductions would then decline and taxable income would rise just when the future earning prospects of the firm are becoming most suspect. As a practical matter, it would be impossible to sort out the various reasons why the market value of a firm's debt is changing.

The adjustment of interest deductions on home mortgages raises other practical problems. Homeowners would have to subtract from their current interest deductions the decline in the real value of the mortgage they owed. In some years, the reduction in the value of the mortgage might exceed the interest payment, cancelling out the interest deduction in full and forcing homeowners to report part of the decline in the real debt as income. If this approach is used, the recalculation of interest deductions and income comes close to applying an accrual principle to changes in the real value of debt. That is, tax liabilities are affected not just when the debt is repaid but when it is revalued in real terms. Aside from the complex calculations that may be involved, this approach may be regarded as conflicting with the realization concepts underlying the current income tax.

Table 2-3. *Effective Marginal Tax Rates on Investment, by Asset, Industry, Source of Finance, and Owner, 1980*
Percent

Investment	Effective tax rate
Type of asset	
Machinery	17.6
Building	41.1
Inventories	47.0
Industry	
Manufacturing	52.7
Other industry	14.6
Commerce	38.2
Source of finance	
Debt	−16.3
New share issues	91.2
Retained earnings	62.4
Owner of asset	
Households	57.5
Tax-exempt institutions	−21.5
Insurance companies	23.4
All investments	37.2

Source: Mervyn A. King and Don Fullerton, *The Taxation of Income from Capital: A Comparative Study of the United States, the United Kingdom, Sweden, and West Germany* (University of Chicago Press, 1984), p. 244.

Nor is there agreement on how best to implement workable, if imperfect, rules for indexing interest income and expense. In view of these complications, a strong case can be made for alternative tax rules that would remove the need for any such adjustments. These issues are explored in chapter 4.

Investment Distortions

In 1980 effective rates of tax on different classes of investments varied from 91.2 percent to −21.5 percent (the latter a subsidy rather than a tax) among broad investment categories (table 2-3), depending on type of investment good, industry, source of finance, and type of ownership. Within these categories the range of effective tax rates was even wider, varying from 111 percent on buildings in either manufacturing or commerce financed by new shares sold to households to −105 percent on machinery used in the commercial sector financed by debt sold to tax-exempt institutions.[27] Since 1980, effective tax rates have dropped,

27. King and Fullerton, *Taxation of Income from Capital*, pp. 299–300.

because inflation has declined and Congress has accelerated depreciation deductions, but disparities in tax rates among types of investment remain large.[28] According to the Treasury Department, the current effective rate of corporation tax on equity-financed investments ranges from -8 percent on equipment eligible for three-year depreciation to 40 percent on structures eligible for eighteen-year depreciation.[29]

These variations in effective tax rates arise because of the interactions of several features of the tax system:

—Tax depreciation bears little relation to true economic depreciation. Investments that owners can "write-off" long before the end of their useful lives are heavily favored relative to investments whose tax lives approximate their economic lives.

—The full investment tax credit is available only on eligible equipment. These assets are favored relative to investments in structures and inventories on which the credit is not available.

—Effective tax rates on investments are sensitive to the tax rates of both the owner of the asset and the supplier of funds for the investment. If there is a difference, income can be directed to the low-bracket taxpayer and expenses to the high-bracket taxpayer, resulting in very low or even negative effective tax rates. For example, a high-bracket owner can borrow to finance investments and receive the full value of deductions for depreciation and interest expense at his or her tax rate, while the lender is taxed on the interest income, often at considerably lower rates.

—Both personal and corporate taxes must be paid on income from corporate sources but only personal taxes on business income from noncorporate sources.

28. For a discussion of changes in the level and dispersion of effective tax rates before and after 1980, see Don Fullerton and Yolanda Kodrzycki Henderson, "Incentive Effects of Taxes on Income from Capital: Alternative Policies in the 1980's," in Charles R. Hulten and Isabel V. Sawhill, eds., *The Legacy of Reaganomics: Prospects for Long-Term Growth* (Washington, D.C.: Urban Institute, 1984), pp. 45–89.

29. These estimates assume 5 percent inflation and a real return after tax of 4 percent. If prices are stable, the effective rates range from -90 percent to 28 percent. These estimates do not take account of the source of funds or ownership of the investment, both of which King and Fullerton showed to be important influences on effective tax rates. See Treasury, *Tax Reform*, vol. 1, p. 107.

—The interaction of the tax code with inflation increases these distortions.

To prevent tax-induced distortions, the effective tax rate on all investments would have to be identical. To achieve this result, Congress would have to reform depreciation deductions, repeal or modify the investment tax credit, adopt tax rules that are not sensitive to inflation, and reduce the difference between the tax imposed on corporate investment and that imposed on noncorporate investment.

Distortions of Consumption and Saving

Wide variations in the taxation of asset income distort household saving. Some asset income—interest, dividends, royalties, and profits—is fully taxed in the year earned. Other asset income is partially taxed. For example, only 40 percent of realized long-term capital gains are taxed. Income on tax-sheltered savings through qualified pension plans, IRAs, and Keoghs is taxed only when withdrawn. And some asset income—on state and local securities, capital gains held until death, and up to $125,000 of gain on a principal residence—is never subject to income tax at all. This variation in the taxation of asset income distorts savings decisions in two ways.

FUTURE CONSUMPTION. First, the taxation of capital income at any positive rate reduces the spending opportunities of people who wish to consume in the future by a larger fraction than it does the spending opportunities of people who wish to consume income as it is earned. A tax on capital income thus distorts personal decisions about when to consume. Table 2-1 demonstrates this problem.

COMPOSITION OF SAVING. The variation in tax rates among assets also distorts household decisions about which assets to hold. In the pursuit of tax advantages, individuals may buy assets that are less productive (in other words, do not have as high a before-tax rate of return), riskier, or less liquid than would otherwise be desirable.

For example, suppose a saver is able to invest in either a tax-exempt investment yielding 8 percent or a fully taxable bond yielding 12 percent. In the absence of tax considerations, the saver would normally choose the latter. And if the tax-exempt borrower were unwilling to pay lenders as much as 12 percent, the saver's decision would direct resources to the activity yielding the higher rate of return. In the presence of taxes, it makes sense for any taxpayer subject to a marginal tax rate of more than 33⅓ percent to invest in the tax-exempt security, thereby misallocating savings to relatively low productivity uses.

Even a taxpayer who does no additional saving but borrows the money to buy tax-exempt securities contributes to such resource misallocations by mobilizing the saving of others. Suppose that an upper-bracket taxpayer subject to a 50 percent rate is able to borrow at 12 percent to buy a tax-exempt security yielding 8 percent; the net cost of the 12 percent loan after deducting interest expenses is only 6 percent, leaving an after-tax profit of 2 percent on the investment. The upper-bracket taxpayer is doing no net saving but is merely borrowing and lending. The saving may be done by a low-bracket taxpayer who lends his or her savings at interest. This example illustrates the sad fact that even if taxes do not induce low-bracket savers to misallocate their savings to low productivity uses, high-bracket taxpayers, who face larger incentives, may do the job for them. As noted earlier, investments that produce capital gains offer similar possibilities. The Internal Revenue Code contains provisions designed to discourage the use of loans with deductible interest expenses to finance the purchase of tax-exempt securities, but they are not hard to avoid.[30]

SAVING RATES. Some advocates of expenditure-type taxes claim that deferring taxes on all asset income until it is used would increase household saving and that this is a major argument against the annual income tax. We agree that tax changes could significantly increase household saving and that such an increase would contribute modestly to economic growth.

If we wish to increase national saving, however, there are more powerful and direct means of reaching this goal. The increase in national saving from tax inducements to encourage household saving would be small relative to the increase in national saving that could be achieved

30. Many holders of tax-exempt securities also are debtors, as shown by Mervyn A. King and Jonathan I. Leap, "Wealth and Portfolio Compositon: Theory and Evidence," Discussion Paper 68 (Economic and Social Research Council Programme, September 1984). Deductibility of interest is unlikely to be questioned if the proceeds of loans are used in the first instance for accepted purposes. Readers of this book who own tax-exempt securities, either directly or through mutual funds or trusts, should ask themselves whether they are deducting interest payments on any form of debt, including a home mortgage; if so, they are, in effect, using borrowed funds to finance holdings of tax-exempt securities and are violating the spirit, if not the letter, of the law. On this issue generally, see Harvey Galper and Eugene Steuerle, "Tax Incentives for Saving," *Brookings Review*, vol. 2 (Winter 1983), pp. 16–23.

by fiscal policies to reduce the deficit or to create a surplus. National saving is the sum of saving by households, business, and government. In recent years household saving has run at 3.5 to 4.5 percent of gross national product. But the federal government has been dissaving about 5 percent of GNP, and the fraction is not projected to fall for the rest of the 1980s.[31] Even if tax changes boosted household saving by about one-third—a decidedly generous estimate—the effect on national saving would be small compared with the direct and certain effects of eliminating the federal deficit.

The tax system should be designed to be fair, conducive to the efficient use of resources, and easy to administer. Any increase in saving would be a positive but minor bonus from reforms that should be adopted only if wholly justified for these other, more important reasons.

Compliance and Administration

Tax laws are not self-enforcing. Taxpayers must go to the trouble and expense of calculating how much they owe. The government must spend part of the proceeds of the tax to collect it and to enforce it, although administrative costs—about one-half percent of revenues collected— are not high. But despite the best efforts of a professional staff of tax administrators at the Internal Revenue Service, taxpayers illegally *evade* part of the taxes they owe. More important, they go to enormous trouble and expense rearranging their affairs legally to *avoid* taxes.

Enforcement is hard to measure, but fragmentary data suggest that it may have declined. Total administrative expenditures of the Internal Revenue Service fell from 0.54 percent of revenues collected in 1975 to 0.41 percent in 1981 before recovering to 0.48 percent in 1984; the ratio of IRS employees to total returns filed dropped by 19 percent over this same period. Although automation and computerized procedures may account for part of these declines, they do not account for the cutback by more than one-third in the proportion of returns audited, from 2.3 percent in 1975 to 1.3 percent in 1984.[32] Administrative efficiency may

31. *Economic Report of the President, 1985*, p. 262.
32. For administrative expenditures see Internal Revenue Service, *Annual Report of the Commissioner and Chief Counsel of the Internal Revenue Service, 1984*, table 22; for ratio of employees to total returns see ibid., tables 6 and 22; and for number of returns audited see ibid., table 7.

have increased, but enforcement of the income tax, at least as measured by audits, has not intensified.

Tax reform holds out hope of improving compliance through two separate routes—reducing marginal tax rates and simplifying the system. Simplification in turn takes two forms: "legal simplification," which would ease taxpayer comprehension, compliance, and administration; and "transactional simplification," which is the reduction of the number and complexity of transactions undertaken to avoid taxes.

Factors Affecting Compliance

MARGINAL RATES. The payoff to tax avoidance or evasion increases with the marginal tax rate, which is the rate at which an additional dollar of taxable income will be taxed or the saving from shielding an additional dollar of income from tax.[33] Although personal income taxes as a percent of personal income (which includes taxable and nontaxable income) have not risen much during the last twenty years, and the maximum marginal tax rate under the personal income tax declined from 70 percent to 50 percent, the marginal tax rate of taxpayers with average income rose until 1981. The increase in the typical marginal tax rate has made tax avoidance increasingly profitable.[34]

COMPLEXITY. While the intensity of enforcement seems to have been falling, opportunities for tax avoidance or evasion have undoubtedly increased because of the growing complexity of the tax code and the increase in inflation. Complexity is responsible for the fact that more than 40 percent of individuals now seek professional help in preparing their tax returns. Even in the case of the so-called short form, almost one-fourth of returns are filed with professional assistance.[35]

Opportunities for tax avoidance have expanded because inflation and high nominal rates of return have increased the proportion of

33. For estimates of the effects of changes in marginal rates on evasion, see Charles T. Clotfelter, "Tax Evasion and Tax Rates: An Analysis of Individual Returns," *Review of Economics and Statistics*, vol. 65 (August 1983), pp. 363–74.

34. Robert J. Barro and Chaipat Sahasakul, "Measuring the Average Marginal Tax Rate from the Individual Income Tax," *Journal of Business*, vol. 56 (October 1983), pp. 419–52. Also, see Eugene Steuerle and Michael Hartzmark, "Individual Income Taxation, 1947–79,"*National Tax Journal*, vol. 34 (June 1981), pp. 145–66.

35. Dorothea Riley, "Individual Income Tax Returns: Selected Characteristics from the 1983 Taxpayer Usage Study," *SOI Bulletin*, vol. 4 (Summer 1984), p. 50.

ordinary income that can be converted into long-term capital gains and thereby deferred and taxed at lower rates. The great acceleration of depreciation deductions in 1981 also contributed to tax shelter opportunities.

The proliferation of tax shelter investments since 1981 illustrates the use of these provisions. Typically, a group of taxpayers is brought together in a partnership to invest in a project yielding large depreciation and interest deductions during the early years and capital gains later. The deductions may save the investors more in taxes than they invested in the project. In such cases, the project may be highly profitable on an after-tax basis even if it never generates capital gains and loses money before tax. These projects are usually marketed only to taxpayers who are in tax brackets of 40 percent or more.

Most of the projects are entirely legal. Some projects are questionable or clearly illegal, and some taxpayers may invest in them intentionally, realizing that an audit is improbable and a successful court challenge less likely still. The laws of chance dictate that a taxpayer who stands to save $100,000 in taxes from a questionable or illegal tax shelter and anticipates legal fees of $50,000 in defending it will come out ahead if there is at least one chance in two that the shelter will be sustained. Only a taxpayer's conscience or his reluctance to face annoying or costly proceedings will deter such questionable practices.

Fortunately, most taxpayers do not calculate so coldly. Such practices are spreading, however, and they are increasingly straining the audit capabilities of the Internal Revenue Service. From 1979 to 1984 the number of returns under examination for tax shelter questions rose from 183,000 to 331,000,[36] with no comparable increase in total IRS staff. As taxpayers devote more resources to avoiding taxes, tax authorities must either increase expenditures on enforcement or watch the quality of administration deteriorate.

Administration of the corporation income tax also poses serious problems. Businesses continue to get bigger and more complex; as subsidiaries proliferate and their international transactions expand, administrative problems multiply. The scope of the problem is hinted at by the fact that in 1984, audits of 4,600 of the 6,500 corporations with assets of more than $100 million yielded recommendations for $7.1 billion in additional taxes.[37]

36. IRS, *Annual Report, 1980*, p. 27; *1984*, p. 13.
37. IRS, *Annual Report, 1984*, p. 60.

Improving Compliance

The key to improving compliance and enforcement is a combination of lower marginal tax rates and understandable rules. For a given amount of revenue, the only way to hold down marginal tax rates is to broaden the tax base by lowering or eliminating deductions, credits, and exclusions. Most personal and corporation tax reforms examined in the following chapters would broaden the tax bases considerably.

Reducing the opportunities for tax avoidance hinges crucially on how income from capital is taxed. In this connection, most reforms would reduce incentives for individuals and business to engage in complex maneuvers just to avoid taxes. The cost to individuals and business from arranging such schemes is enormous and is not captured by estimates of administrative costs or even of the time and money taxpayers spend in filling out forms. Managerial talent and time is diverted from efforts to increase productivity, develop new products, and expand markets, to a search for ways to avoid taxes. As noted above, any system that makes tax liabilities depend on the time when income is realized and that imposes widely varying tax rates on different kinds of receipts makes tax manipulation a tempting and rewarding pastime. In these circumstances, a misallocation of scarce talent to concoct such privately beneficial but socially unproductive schemes is inevitable.

Implementing the New Tax Design

It is much easier to design a new tax system from scratch than to reform an old one. The goal of both tax design and reform is to achieve a fair, efficient, and administrable system. But the shift from the old system to the new will cause two sorts of problems. First, it will alter asset values and change the relative economic status of businesses and of individuals. Second, it will require transition rules to reduce such disruptions or to spread them over time.

Losses from Rule Changes

People have made many economic arrangements under the assumption (or hope) that the current tax law will remain in effect. Although everyone realizes that the permanence of the existing tax system is not assured, taxpayers stoutly resist new tax provisions that "change the rules in midstream," particularly ones that threaten losses. Consider, for example, the effect on investors of terminating the deductibility of mortgage interest and property taxes on owner-occupied housing, the exclusion from tax of interest on debt of state and local governments, the exclusion of 60 percent of capital gains on assets held more than six months, the forgiveness of tax on capital gains held until death, the allowance of depreciation deductions larger than true economic depreciation, the deductibility of interest in excess of capital income, the investment tax credit, and the general policy of taxing nominal rather than real income.

Tax changes of this magnitude typically will increase substantially the taxes that some people and businesses must pay. It is little wonder that vigorous opposition to such changes obstructs large-scale tax reform. If the proposed tax reform improves overall economic efficiency, however, aggregate output will be larger after the changes than before, and gains will exceed losses. But potential gainers and losers will not necessarily exert equal influence on the final outcome. Those who would benefit from new investment opportunities but do not fully appreciate the advantages of the new rules may be indifferent to change. In contrast, those who think they will suffer large losses will make disproportionate efforts to fight change. Furthermore, concentrated losses induced by policy changes are widely regarded as unfair.[38]

Transition

Various steps could be taken to soften the effect of tax changes on asset values. For example, interest on state and local bonds is now tax exempt; making all such interest taxable would lower the price of municipal bonds, imposing capital losses on owners of outstanding issues who sold their securities before maturity and income losses on owners who continued to hold them. Applying the new rules only to securities issued after a certain date, such as when the new tax law is officially proposed or enacted, would fully protect, and might even reward, owners of outstanding and increasingly scarce tax-exempt bonds. But it would not help state and local governments, which would abruptly face in-

---

38. See Martin S. Feldstein, "Compensation in Tax Reform," *National Tax Journal*, vol. 29 (June 1976), pp. 123–30; and Feldstein, "On the Theory of Tax Reform," *Journal of Public Economics*, vol. 6 (July–August 1976), pp. 77–104.

creased interest costs on new debt issues. To meet this problem, some have proposed direct federal subsidies to state and local governments sufficient to compensate them for the increase in interest costs they would face should their interest payments become taxable.

The case of tax-exempt bonds teaches three lessons: transitional rules can protect or compensate those who lose from tax reform. Such rules may add to complexity, and the payment of compensation reduces the net addition to revenues from tax reform. In this example, taxpayers and the Internal Revenue Service would have to account separately for interest paid on bonds issued before and after the effective date. Also, if a permanent subsidy were paid to state and local governments, much of the added revenue from taxing their interest payments would finance the subsidy and would be unavailable for reducing tax rates.[39]

Reducing the favorable treatment of owner-occupied housing would raise even more serious transitional problems. Most Americans live in houses they own. They would fight tax changes that lower house values unless such rules were an essential component of a plan beneficial to them on balance.

A similar problem surrounds reform of depreciation deductions and the investment tax credit. Replacing these provisions with neutral rules for capital cost recovery would change the composition of investment. For this reason a new and neutral system should be phased in gradually and accompanied by monetary policies to sustain overall investment.

Although transition problems are difficult, they should not permanently bar tax reform. The tax code is not constitutionally guaranteed, and no business or individual can be protected against all consequences of change. But some gains and losses are so large that they cannot be ignored. The traditional principles of taxation must be broadened to include concern for the problems of transition in developing feasible and desirable tax reform.

39. It appears at first glance that states and localities would suffer increased interest costs unless the subsidy absorbed all of the extra revenue. Such an inference would be incorrect if after-tax yields on taxable and tax-exempt bonds are equalized at some marginal tax rate below the top bracket rate, and some bonds are held by people above this break-even tax rate. In that event, a direct subsidy will cost less than taxation of interest payments will yield. See, for example, Susan Ackerman and David Ott, "An Analysis of the Revenue Effects of Proposed Substitutes for Tax Exemption of State and Local Bonds," *National Tax Journal*, vol. 23 (December 1970), pp. 397–406; and Harvey Galper and John Petersen, "An Analysis of Subsidy Plans to Support State and Local Borrowing," *National Tax Journal*, vol. 24 (June 1971), pp. 205–34, especially pp. 229–30.

Options for the Future

The current personal income tax gets poor marks for fairness, efficiency, and simplicity. It is unfair because it imposes different tax burdens on people who have the same capacity to spend. It taxes some forms of compensation to labor but not others. And it provides a deduction for some forms of saving but not others.

It is inefficient because it distorts the timing and composition of consumption. It imposes widely varying rates of tax on income from different types of capital. It diverts capital from its most productive uses, thereby reducing economic efficiency and retarding growth. And although some of these variations are rationalized on the ground that they promote important national objectives in addition to collecting revenue, the claims are undermined by the wastefulness of most such provisions in promoting those objectives.

The income tax is cumbersome for taxpayers and administrators alike. The proliferation of credits, deductions, allowances, and exclusions has expanded opportunities for tax avoidance; and increases in the marginal tax rates of the average taxpayer have raised the profit from pursuing them. As a result, the administrative burden on the Internal Revenue Service has increased, although its administrative resources have not. In their efforts to avoid taxes, individuals and businesses divert time and money from socially productive activities. If these trends continue, the sense among taxpayers that most people are paying their fair share will collapse. This sense of fairness is essential for the continued self-assessment of the income tax.

In the next two chapters, we examine alternative ways to reform the income tax. Chapter 3 describes and evaluates three large-scale reform plans, one by Treasury, one by leading Democrats, and one by leading Republicans. These plans share with the current system the principle that taxes should be based on annual realized income. Chapter 4 describes a cash flow income tax on all uses of income—consumption plus wealth transfers through gift or bequest—which would base tax liabilities on lifetime income. The reforms examined in chapters 3 and 4 would deal in varying degrees with the shortcomings of the present tax system. The magnitude of the changes examined in each chapter is similar. In each case the reforms would cause significant changes in the relative valuation of capital goods, and transitional rules would require close attention.

CHAPTER THREE

Rebuilding the Income Tax

THE INCOME TAX can be made vastly fairer and simpler without altering its fundamental structure. Some of the important problems examined in chapter 2 would remain. But this fact should not obscure the importance of the gains that are possible. To achieve these gains, however, Congress would have to enact numerous reforms that have been strenuously and successfully resisted in the past.

This chapter focuses on three major recent proposals to improve the current annual income tax: one offered by the Treasury Department in November 1984; one by Senator Bill Bradley (Democrat of New Jersey) and Representative Richard A. Gephardt (Democrat of Missouri), advanced originally in 1983; and one by Representative Jack F. Kemp (Republican of New York) and Senator Bob Kasten (Republican of Wisconsin), first introduced in 1984 and then significantly revised in 1985.[1] We describe these plans, point out the major improvements they would achieve, and then describe the major problems that no income tax based on the annual taxation of realized incomes can solve.

The Plans Summarized

The Treasury, Bradley-Gephardt, and Kemp-Kasten proposals all would eliminate most personal deductions, many business deductions, and most credits. By thus broadening the tax base, each could sharply lower rates from today's levels while collecting the same amount of revenue. Each proposal would reduce the number of tax brackets; each is also concerned with maintaining roughly today's distribution of tax burdens across income classes. The Treasury and Bradley-Gephardt

1. These proposals are undergoing repeated revisions. The descriptions in this chapter reflect their main features in early 1985 as they would apply to taxpayers in 1986. Current law is also described as it would apply in 1986. See the Internal Revenue Code of 1954, as amended.

proposals succeed in maintaining the average effective tax rate of each income class—the ratio of the class's tax liabilities to economic income; of course, some individual taxpayers within each income class would pay more taxes, some less, but the average effective rate of each class would not be significantly changed. In contrast, the Kemp-Kasten plan succeeds in maintaining distributional neutrality only for income classes up to $100,000. At higher incomes, effective tax rates under Kemp-Kasten are lower than those under current law.[2] Though similar in these broad outlines, these proposals differ in economically significant ways.

The Treasury Plan

The Treasury Department plan would greatly broaden the tax base and reduce marginal tax rates by repealing or limiting many of today's itemized deductions.[3] As a result, the proportion of taxpayers who find it advantageous to itemize deductions would fall from 36 percent to less than 25 percent. Correcting the measurement of capital income to take account of inflation would bring taxable income considerably closer to real economic income than it is now. These changes would simplify compliance and discourage investments undertaken to avoid or defer tax. Here is the plan in more detail.

DEDUCTIONS ELIMINATED. The proposal eliminates the following provisions: personal deductions for all state and local taxes, including property taxes by homeowners; deductions for charitable contributions of up to 2 percent of income; and employer deductions for fringe benefits other than qualified pension plans.

DEDUCTIONS RETAINED. It retains deductions for mortgage interest on

2. The distributional neutrality of these proposals is based on the assumption that economic behavior would be the same after reform as it is under current law. Since each proposal calls for far-reaching changes, this assumption cannot be correct. Except for a few provisions that have clearly identifiable behavioral incentives, however, this assumption is reasonable for estimates of the immediate effects of reforms on revenues. We indicate below some provisions for which the effect on behavior is so obvious and gross that the effects on revenues cannot be ignored. Also, the traditional calculation of tax burdens does not take into account the substantial changes in *before-tax* incomes resulting from current law tax preferences or from revisions of these preferences. For a discussion of this issue, see Harvey Galper and Eric Toder, "Transfer Elements in the Taxation of Income from Capital," in Marilyn Moon, ed., *Economic Transfers in the United States* (University of Chicago Press, 1984), pp. 87–138.

3. U.S. Department of the Treasury, *Tax Reform for Fairness, Simplicity, and Economic Growth: The Treasury Department Report to the President*, 3 vols. (Treasury Department, 1984).

a primary residence, charitable contributions in excess of 2 percent of income, and contributions to Keogh plans and individual retirement accounts (IRAs). The limit on contributions to IRAs would be increased from $2,000 to $2,500 for workers and from $250 to $2,500 for spouses who do not work outside the home.

EXCLUSIONS ELIMINATED. It eliminates the exclusion of interest on tax-exempt securities issued for other than governmental purposes; these securities now constitute 62 percent of long-term tax-exempt bonds issued. Income now excluded that would become taxable includes military allowances for quarters and subsistence; unemployment compensation; disability payments from workers' compensation, black lung, and veterans' programs; scholarships and fellowships in excess of tuition and incidental expenses; prizes and awards; and employer-purchased health insurance in excess of stipulated amounts and all group term life insurance.

TAX-FREE INCOME LEVEL INCREASED. It nearly doubles personal exemptions, from $1,090 to $2,000. It replaces the extra exemptions for the elderly and the blind and the credit for the elderly with an expanded credit. This new credit, together with the higher personal exemptions, would slightly increase tax-free income levels for the elderly. The plan would increase the zero-bracket amount (or standard deduction) for single persons from $2,510 to $2,800 and for joint filers from $3,710 to $3,800. Tax free income levels would rise from $9,613 to $11,800 for a one earner couple with two children.

TAX RATES CUT. It sharply reduces tax rates on both individuals and corporations. Individual joint filers would pay tax at 15 percent on the first $28,000 of income in excess of tax-free levels, 25 percent on the next $32,000, and 35 percent on income greater than $60,000. Single persons would pay the same rates as joint filers but with the cutoffs at the first $16,500 of income in excess of tax-free levels, the next $18,800, and income greater than $35,300, respectively.

INDEXING EXPANDED. It retains indexing of tax brackets, personal exemptions, and the zero bracket amount. In addition, it would make exact inflation adjustments for capital gains, depreciation, and inventories and approximate adjustments for interest receipts and expenses.[4]

INVESTMENT PREFERENCES REPEALED. It repeals the accelerated cost recovery system enacted in 1981 and the investment tax credit and replaces them with schedules designed to measure true economic depre-

---

4. The treatment of interest is described in some detail below.

ciation. It would also repeal most special business deductions other than for cost of goods sold.

DIVIDEND TAXATION EASED. The proposal lowers the corporate rate from a maximum of 46 percent to a flat 33 percent. To reduce the double taxation of dividends, the plan would allow corporations to deduct from corporate taxable income one-half of dividends paid to domestic individual shareholders and to foreign shareholders residing in countries with which the United States has bilateral tax treaties.

CAPITAL GAINS TAXED. It repeals the 60 percent preferential exclusion of long-term capital gains. Together with the 35 percent top rate on individuals, repeal would increase the maximum rate on nominal gains from 20 percent under current law to 35 percent. However, the indexing provisions would reduce taxes on gains except where the appreciation of asset values much exceeds the increase in the price level.[5]

FINANCIAL INSTITUTIONS AFFECTED. Banks would no longer be allowed to deduct interest costs incurred to finance the purchase of tax-exempt securities. Increases in the cash value of life insurance would be imputed as taxable income to individual policyholders.

The Bradley-Gephardt Plan

Like the Treasury plan, the Bradley-Gephardt proposal greatly broadens the base of the personal and corporation income taxes, sharply reduces tax rates, and reduces the number of individual income tax brackets.[6] Under the plan, 80 percent of all individual taxpayers are subject to a flat rate of 14 percent. Also like the Treasury proposal, Bradley-Gephardt eliminates the distinction between capital gains and ordinary income, although it includes nominal rather than real gains in the tax base.

DEDUCTIONS ELIMINATED. The proposal eliminates most itemized deductions, credits, and exclusions for individuals.

DEDUCTIONS RETAINED. It would retain extra personal exemptions for the blind and elderly; deductions for mortgage interest, charitable contributions, state income and local property taxes, contributions to IRAs and Keogh plans, and employee business expenses; the exclusion of some transfer payments; and the exclusion of interest on state or local general obligation bonds.

5. A 35 percent tax on the real gain is less than a 20 percent tax on the nominal gain if the real gain is less than 4/7 (or 57 percent) of the nominal gain.
6. S. 409, H.R. 800.

ALL CAPITAL GAINS TAXED. It repeals exclusion of 60 percent of long-term capital gains for both individuals and corporations. Given the maximum marginal rate of 30 percent, repeal increases the maximum rate on capital gains from 20 percent under current law to 30 percent, slightly lower than the 35 percent maximum rate proposed by the Treasury. Bradley-Gephardt, however, does not adjust capital gains for inflation.

TAX-FREE LEVELS INCREASED. It increases exemptions for the taxpayer and the taxpayer's spouse from $1,090 per person under current law to $1,600; it leaves exemptions for other dependents unchanged. It increases the zero-bracket amount to $6,000 for joint returns and $3,000 for other taxpayers. In combination, these two provisions increase tax-free income levels for a family of four from $9,613 to $11,200.

TAX RATES CUT. The individual tax schedule begins with a basic rate of 14 percent on income *less deductions* up to $40,000 per year for joint returns and $25,000 per year for other taxpayers. An additional tax of 12 percent would be imposed on *total* income, without deductions, of $40,000 to $65,000 for joint returns and $25,000 to $37,500 for other taxpayers. An additional tax of 16 percent would be imposed on total incomes, without deductions, greater than these amounts.

INDEXING REPEALED. It repeals automatic inflation adjustments of tax brackets, personal exemptions, and the zero-bracket amount of the individual income tax and allows no adjustments for inflation in the calculation of capital gains, depreciation, or interest.

INVESTMENT PREFERENCES REPEALED. It eliminates most business deductions, credits, and allowances for particular types of investment. Deductions for ordinary business expenses would be retained. It repeals the investment tax credit and allows deductions for depreciation on much less accelerated schedules than under current law. These schedules approximate economic depreciation at an inflation rate of 6 percent.

CORPORATE RATE LOWERED. It taxes corporate income at 30 percent, the same as the top individual rate.

The Kemp-Kasten Plan

Like the Treasury and Bradley-Gephardt plans, the Kemp-Kasten proposal eliminates most deductions and credits, reduces rates, and narrows their range.[7]

7. S. 325, H.R. 777.

TAX-FREE LEVELS INCREASED. The plan increases personal exemptions from $1,090 to $2,000 for the taxpayer, spouse, and all dependents and repeals the extra exemptions for the aged and blind. It increases the zero bracket amount from $2,510 to $2,600 for single taxpayers but reduces it from $3,710 to $3,300 for joint returns. However, it raises tax-free income levels for a family of four from $9,613 to $14,125.

SELECTED DEDUCTIONS RETAINED. The plan eliminates most personal deductions but retains those for charitable contributions, mortgage interest, real property taxes, and medical expenses greater than 10 percent of income.

TAX RATES CUT. The plan taxes four-fifths of earnings up to the social security maximum ($41,400 in 1986) at a rate of 24 percent, making the effective tax rate 19.2 percent. This range includes all the earnings of more than 90 percent of wage earners. Above the social security maximum, the effective tax rate on earned income would jump to 28.8 percent. This increase would result first from taking back the earnings exclusion at the rate of 20 cents for each dollar of earnings, and, second, when the exclusion is wholly eliminated, from increasing taxable income by 20 percent of earnings. The corporation income tax rate would be reduced to 15 percent on profits of $50,000 or less, 25 percent on profits between $50,000 and $100,000, and 35 percent on profits greater than $100,000.

EARNED INCOME CREDIT REDUCED. The earned income credit is now 11 percent of the first $5,000 of earnings and is phased out based on income from $6,500 to $11,000. The Kemp-Kasten proposal would increase the maximum credit to 15 percent of the first $4,000 of earnings but would phase it out completely by the time income reaches $8,000.

INDEXING EXTENDED. It keeps automatic inflation adjustments for the personal exemption and zero-bracket amounts. In addition, it would adjust capital gains and depreciation for inflation. For capital gains, it would allow taxpayers each year to choose the 40 percent exclusion or an inflation adjustment, whichever would be more favorable. Unlike the Treasury proposal, Kemp-Kasten makes no inflation adjustments for inventories or interest income and expense.

ACCELERATED DEPRECIATION MODIFIED. The plan repeals the investment tax credit and modifies the accelerated depreciation rules introduced in 1981 (the Accelerated Cost Recovery System). The new rules would provide the equivalent to immediate write off, or expensing, of all depreciable assets.

LIFE INSURANCE AFFECTED. The plan taxes as personal income additions to the cash value of life insurance.

Problems Solved

The reduction of marginal tax rates is the biggest achievement of base-broadening tax reforms. Lower rates curtail the tax-induced distortions of labor supply, saving, investment, and risk taking.

The next big potential advantage of base-broadening is that it can reduce investment distortions caused by wide variations in effective tax rates on capital income. Reductions in such distortions would result in economywide gains in efficiency from an improved allocation of capital. The three plans realize this potential in varying degrees. Treasury and Bradley-Gephardt reform depreciation deductions. Kemp-Kasten also changes depreciation rules but treats various assets inconsistently. Treasury provides full indexing. Kemp-Kasten takes a piecemeal approach. All three eliminate the investment tax credit and special deductions, other credits, exclusions, and allowances for particular types of investment. The Treasury plan goes farthest in removing investment distortions; Bradley-Gephardt also makes considerable progress; Kemp-Kasten removes some existing distortions but, as indicated below, increases others in potentially damaging ways.

Taxing currently exempt fringe benefits would bring other efficiency gains. Without tax inducements to adopt particular kinds of benefit packages, employees and employers would be encouraged to base negotiations about the mix of cash compensation and fringe benefits on actual social costs, not on tax considerations.

Eliminating many special deductions and credits simplifies tax compliance in two important ways. First, it reduces the direct costs of compliance because taxpayers confront a simpler tax form and need to keep fewer records. Fewer people, for example, would find it profitable to go to the trouble of itemizing deductions. The second and far more important simplification flows from the reduction of incentives to arrange one's affairs—make special investments or negotiate unusual forms of compensation, for example—to shelter economic income from tax. Only the most obvious of these arrangements are called tax shelters. But many business mergers, investments, deferred compensation agreements, and sheltered saving plans are undertaken not because they add to economic productivity but because they generate deductions or credits that reduce or defer tax.

All three proposals reduce the number of tax brackets. Under Bradley-Gephardt 80 percent of all taxpayers would face a 14 percent rate. Under

Kemp Kasten taxpayers would face a tax rate of either 19.2 percent or 28.8 percent on earned income and all would face a rate of 24 percent on other income. Taxpayers would not have to concern themselves with wide variations in tax rates as their income changed. Under the Treasury proposal only a small proportion of taxpayers would face tax rates greater than 25 percent.

If most taxpayers face a single rate, then the deductions still remaining in these plans have the same value for most people. Under present law, the tax saving from deductions for mortgage interest, for example, ranges from 11 cents per dollar of mortgage interest for low-bracket taxpayers to 50 cents per dollar, almost five times as much, for high-bracket taxpayers. Under Bradley-Gephardt, all taxpayers would save 14 cents tax per dollar of deduction; under Kemp-Kasten the single statutory rate saves all taxpayers 24 cents per dollar of deduction; and under the Treasury proposal the range would be from 15 to 35 cents. To the extent that the government encourages homeownership or charitable giving through such deductions, all three proposals would provide more nearly equal incentives.[8]

Of the three proposals examined in this chapter, the Treasury proposal by a wide margin is the most far reaching, because it attempts to correct distortions that arise from the fundamental characteristics of an annual income tax based on realizations. As we have seen, the most troublesome problems under the annual income tax concern the taxation of capital income. It is in this area that the three plans exhibit their most significant differences, particularly as a result of Treasury's proposals for comprehensive adjustments for inflation and for partial integration of individual and corporate taxes.

A Critique of Comprehensive Income Tax Reform

Base-broadening tax reform along the lines of the three plans described here can claim great progress in reducing the vast number of deductions,

8. Some tax deductions may best be regarded not as subsidies but as allowances for involuntary expenditures that reduce discretionary income. Such expenditures should be deducted from income before tax is calculated, although to simplify compliance, deductions might be allowed only to the extent that they exceed some fraction of income. Health expenditures are perhaps the best example of such involuntary outlays. From this perspective, the treatment of health expenses in the Bradley Gephardt proposal is incorrect. By permitting the deduction of health outlays only against the first bracket rate of 14 percent, that proposal would have the effect of converting the deduction into a 14 percent credit.

credits, and exclusions that infest the tax code and that are popularly seen as the main problem with the tax system. But there are four problems—accrued versus realized income, inflation effects, corporate double taxation, and distortion of saving—that are not solved by the three plans. These four problems are more serious than the use of the tax system to promote nonrevenue objectives. Each of these problems generates inequities and inefficiencies, and each has spawned special measures to offset these effects. Such palliatives, however, create additional distortions. None of the proposed reforms of the annual income tax solves all of these structural problems.

Accrual versus Realization

As discussed in chapter 2, income is an accrual concept. Accretions to wealth, whether or not realized in cash, add to one's spendable income. With a few exceptions, however, taxes are and must be based on realizations—that is, on actual transactions. This contradiction between what income means and how it must be measured produces complexity, inefficiency, and inequities that cannot be removed from any annual income tax.

The treatment of capital gains highlights the problem. By the definition of income, unrealized capital gains should be taxed as they accrue, for that is when they add to a taxpayer's net worth. But the current tax system, based on the realization principle, imposes tax on capital gains only when an asset is sold. Inflation aside (more on that later), taxing gains only when realized defers tax on appreciation. As a result, income that takes the form of appreciation on assets as diverse as land, apartment houses, corporate stock, and timber is not taxed when earned; rather, tax is collected only when the assets are sold and cash is realized, often years after the income was earned. None of the three plans examined in this chapter modifies this feature of existing law in any significant way.

The benefits of deferral are not small. For corporations subject to a 46 percent tax rate, a cash activity must yield 16.8 percent before tax to be as profitable after tax as an investment yielding 12 percent per year on which tax can be deferred for twenty years.[9] If deferral promoted

9. An investment of $1,000 that yields 12 percent per year will accumulate to $9,646 after twenty years. If the gain of $8,646 is taxed at the full corporate rate of 46 percent, the tax will be $3,977, and the investor will be left with $5,669. If the gain is taxed annually, a 16.8 percent before-tax rate of return will yield an after-tax rate of 9.1

especially meritorious activities, it might be acceptable. But it does not. Further, as noted in chapter 2, the deferral preference is unfair as well as inefficient because it favors taxpayers who have accrued income over those who have realized income.

PRACTICAL PROBLEMS OF REALIZATION. Efforts to alleviate the problems of excluding unrealized income from tax have produced awesome complexity. Artfully crafted distinctions between capital assets and other assets have evolved. These distinctions require the tax code to answer questions that defy logic. What is a capital asset? When does an asset sale generate ordinary income and when does it generate capital gains? How can excessive borrowing against appreciated assets be prevented? What should be done about capital losses? In more general terms: how can the law cope with the full force of human ingenuity bent on converting ordinary income into capital gains?

The tax code permits unlimited deductions of ordinary business expenses by individuals and corporations, even if such deductions result in losses that are used to offset income from other sources. But individual taxpayers can offset only $3,000 of net capital losses against ordinary income and corporations can offset capital losses only against capital gains. These limitations on the deduction of capital losses are necessary, as noted in chapter 2, to prevent wealthy taxpayers from manipulating capital transactions to defer tax indefinitely

The resulting arbitrary definitions beget both complexity and endless opportunities for game playing. As shown in chapter 2, for example, two taxpayers in identical economic circumstances may be taxed quite differently depending upon when they decide to realize gains or losses. The simplest way to minimize taxes is to sell assets with losses and hold on to assets with gains, or alternatively to cash out gains by borrowing against appreciated assets. In the latter case, the gains are not taxed, and the interest on the loan is deductible.

Admittedly, some complexity arises from the artificial distinction between long-term and short-term capital gains. But even if long-term gains were fully taxed, a definition of capital assets—those assets

---

percent, assuming a 46 percent tax rate. An investment of $1,000 will accumulate to $5,669 if it is invested at 9.1 percent for twenty years. This example ignores the fact that long-term capital gains are taxed at not more than 28 percent when earned by corporations. If this tax differential is also taken into account, the investment that yields annual taxable income would have to earn 19.2 percent to leave the investor as well off as he or she would be if the investment yielded 12 percent and tax was deferred for twenty years.

generating capital gains and losses as distinct from ordinary income— would still be required, if only to limit offsets of capital losses against ordinary income. Without such limits, many taxpayers could and would avoid all taxes.

All three proposals also continue to rely on arbitrary distinctions among kinds of borrowing at the same time that they try to restrict arbitrage opportunities. The Treasury proposal would disallow personal interest deductions exceeding capital income plus $5,000. Bradley-Gephardt would disallow all interest expenses, other than mortgage interest, in excess of investment income. Kemp-Kasten would disallow deductions for consumer interest but retain deductions for mortgage and investment interest. The goal of these rules is clear, but, like the current rules, they would discriminate among taxpayers with different forms of borrowing and would be vulnerable to financial manipulation.

INTEREST. Accrued but unpaid interest is another problem of an income tax that base-broadening by itself cannot solve. Consider a bond issued for less than its redemption value, say $200, and redeemed some years later for $1,000. The $800 appreciation of the bond is interest in an economic sense even if periodic payments are not made to the bond-holder. If the $800 were taxed only at redemption, the effective tax rate would be much lower than if interest were taxed annually. Because bondholders would prefer tax-deferred income to currently taxable interest, issuers of such bonds might be able to reduce the interest rate they must to pay to attract lenders. The resulting interest rate differences would distort the investment.

Congress recognized this problem and imposed some tax on unpaid accrued interest.[10] Thus, in the above example, a compound rate of interest equivalent to the $800 increase in the bond value can be used to impute interest income to the bondholder and interest expense to the issuer even though no money may change hands.[11]

Unfortunately, not all calculations are so simple. For example, the final value of the bond may be pegged to such other variables as the

10. In 1969, Congress first recognized that the discount on a bond originally issued at less than its final redemption value constitutes interest income to bondholders, and it enacted rules to treat the discount as current interest. Subsequent legislation in 1982 and 1984 tightened these rules and extended them to property that is not publicly traded and, in part, to bonds selling at a market discount.

11. If the $800 were received over a fifteen-year period, this would be equivalent to a compound rate of return of 11.33 percent, generating interest income and expense of $22.65 in the first year, $25.22 in the second year, and $101.77 in the fifteenth year.

consumer price index or to the prime interest rate when the bond matures.[12] It is unclear in such cases exactly what values have accrued at any date before maturity. But if accruals can be calculated only if future values are specified in advance, borrowers would be encouraged to create uncertainty, thereby preventing the calculation of accruals to preserve tax deferral. Although guideline interest rates can be used when final asset values are not known, such practice further removes the tax base from actual transactions and makes it increasingly arbitrary.[13]

Inflation

The second problem with annual income taxation based on nominal values is that it fails to correct distortions of the tax base arising from inflation. As explained in chapter 2, inflation causes mismeasurement of capital gains, depreciation, cost of goods sold from inventory, and interest income and expense. This problem is distinct from the far less important issue of bracket creep—the tendency of inflation to push taxpayers into higher tax brackets even when their real incomes do not change. Bracket creep can be prevented by periodic adjustments in tax rates. But income mismeasurement can be forestalled only if methods of computing taxable income are corrected.

An accurate calculation of real income for tax purposes would require inflation corrections for all four sources of mismeasurement—capital gains, depreciation, inventories, and interest. Even a piecemeal approach could reduce the inefficiencies created by current law. For example, indexing capital gains, but not other elements of capital income, reduces tax distortions.[14] But the Kemp-Kasten treatment of gains

12. New York State Bar Association, "Original Issue Discount and Coupon Stripping," *Tax Notes*, vol. 22 (March 5, 1984), pp. 993–1034.

13. It is not surprising to find observers of this scene arguing against cumbersome and inaccurate imputations for accruals and in favor of cash accounting rules to place all transactions involving the time value of money on a uniform cash or realization basis. See, for example, Mark Stier, "Original Issue Discount Rules and the Time Value of Money," *Tax Notes*, vol. 23 (June 4, 1984), pp. 1101–06.

14. The advantage of current law relative to indexing the basis of capital assets financed completely from borrowed funds is equal to

$$(t_i - t_g)G + (t_o - t_i)R - t_iP,$$

where t_o is the current marginal tax rate on ordinary income, t_g is the current marginal tax rate on capital gains, t_i is the marginal tax rate under the indexed system, G is the rate of gain in the value of the asset, R is the nominal rate of interest, and P is the rate of inflation. This expression is positive for current values of t_g and t_o and for any values aggravates them. Taxpayers can choose between a 40 percent exclusion and full taxation of real gains. For many taxpayers this option is likely to result in taxing a smaller fraction of gains than under current law. Furthermore, it would still be profitable for taxpayers to avoid tax by borrowing funds to buy capital assets, even if the economic return were negative. The Kemp-Kasten proposal also indexes depreciation allowances, but as noted below, they are excessively generous.

The Treasury proposal adjusts all elements of capital income—not only capital gains but also depreciation and inventories. In addition, it makes an approximate adjustment for the effects of inflation on interest income and expense. An exact adjustment would yield real interest, which is the difference between the actual interest rate and the rate of inflation. To calculate a rate of interest, one must know the amount of interest and the value of the asset. But the current value of many assets can only be guessed. Futhermore, calculations would be required for every individual transaction involving interest income or expense. Most taxpayers would find such calculations difficult and all would find them cumbersome.

The Treasury tax plan does not depend on asset values for the determination of how much interest to exclude. Instead, it excludes a fraction of interest income and expense based on an assumed interest rate; actual interest rates play no part in determining the excluded share. The assumed interest rate is 6 percent plus the rate of inflation—for example, with 4 percent inflation, the assumed interest rate is 10 percent. The proportion of the actual interest excluded is the fraction of the assumed interest rate represented by inflation. With 4 percent inflation, therefore, 40 percent of actual interest income and expense is excluded from taxable income. If inflation is 14 percent, the assumed interest rate is 20 percent, and 70 percent of actual interest income and expense is excluded. These fractions apply regardless of the actual interest rate.

The Treasury plan permits individuals to deduct mortgage interest expense on a primary residence and up to $5,000 of other net interest expense without making an inflation adjustment. All net interest income would be adjusted for inflation. Together with the indexation of depreciation, inventories, and capital gains, Treasury's proposed rules for

---

of t_l less than t_o, if the values of G, R, and P are plausible. With such plausible values, only if real interest is sufficiently negative (that is, if inflation is sufficiently higher than the nominal interest rate) will the partially indexed system be more favorable to the fully leveraged investor than current law.

interest indexing are a workable approximation to the measurement of real capital income.

But the interest adjustment is rough at best and could become a focus for new distortions. The Treasury adjustment is incomplete and imprecise for at least three reasons. First, the nonindexation of mortgage interest and up to $5,000 of additional net interest expense perpetuates the incentive to engage in tax arbitrage—the use of borrowed funds on which nominal interest expense is fully deductible to buy assets that yield indexed, and therefore only partially taxed, nominal capital income. This provision is an additional break for homeowners and could increase the existing law's bias toward investment in owner-occupied housing.

Second, the method of excluding a portion of interest is inaccurate in most specific cases and is probably incorrect on the average. Take a specific case. When inflation suddenly rises, the difference between the current inflation rate and the interest rate on outstanding loans negotiated before inflation rose may be less than zero. For example, a loan negotiated at 8 percent may still be outstanding when inflation is 10 percent. Yet the Treasury formula assumes that the interest rate is 6 percent above the inflation rate and thus would still permit such borrowers to deduct part of the interest they are then paying. Under a complete adjustment, no interest would be deductible, and in addition income would be increased in recognition of the decline in the real value of outstanding debt.

To further illustrate, when the inflation rate is 10 percent, the real value of an outstanding loan of $10,000 falls by $1,000 per year. That real decline in debt represents income to the borrower and would be offset against interest deductions under a system of complete inflation adjustments. Consider the taxpayer paying 8 percent interest on the $10,000 loan. Precise income measurements would permit the taxpayer to deduct $800 in interest and report the $1,000 decline in the value of debt as income, resulting in net income of $200.[15] Under the Treasury proposal, the taxpayer would still be permitted a deduction—in this case equal to ⅜ of the $800 interest paid, or $300.[16]

15. Note that this approach breaches the principle that income should be taxed only when realized. The decline in value of the outstanding debt is an accrual. If accruals are to be recognized, the change in the capital value of the debt attributable to the change in interest rates should, in principle, also be taken into account. For the problems with such complete indexing, see chapter 2, especially p. 35, note 26.

16. This calculation is based on an assumed nominal interest rate of 16 percent—

The Treasury's assumed 6 percent real interest rate, although reasonable today, is higher than the real interest rates that have prevailed historically. Unless the assumed real rate were adjusted periodically, taxable interest could substantially exceed actual real interest income, although by less than under current law.

Third, the interest adjustment is conceptually wrong for financial institutions, most of whose profits come from the spread between interest paid on borrowing and received on lending. The loss from erosion of their assets by inflation is matched by the gain from the erosion of their liabilities. The spread between their cost of funds and their returns on lending is their real profit margin and should be taxed in full. Yet, the Treasury inflation adjustment would exclude a portion of the spread, or net interest income, from tax. The result would be simply a subsidy to financial institutions.

Despite these departures from perfection, the Treasury's overall indexing procedures score well when compared with current law. They could score even better if, for example, financial institutions were permitted to index only the portion of their net interest income attributable to equity. In addition, the excessively generous provisions for home mortgage interest could be tightened, for example by capping the deduction. Even as it stands, the Treasury's proposals for indexing are superior to those in Bradley-Gephardt, which do not index any aspect of capital income, and to those in Kemp-Kasten, which do index depreciation, but index capital gains only imperfectly, and inventories and interest not at all.

The successful indexation of capital income can have important economic advantages. Inflation interacts with the current, unindexed tax system to cause systematic biases in investments—for example, away from long-lived investments and in favor of debt-financed investments. Successful indexation would reduce these biases and the resulting inefficiencies.

Indexation should also encourage all investment by reducing uncertainty.[17] High and variable rates of inflation create both general uncer-

---

the guideline real interest rate of 6 percent plus the 10 percent rate of inflation. Under the Treasury procedure and an inflation component of 10 percent, the inclusion fraction would be $\frac{9}{16}$, or $\frac{3}{8}$.

17. When investors undertake a new venture, they face the risk associated with a long-term commitment in an uncertain environment and the financial risk of increases in future tax burdens arising from the interaction between inflation and the tax system.

tainty and tax-burden uncertainty. These high risks tend to deter invest-ment. Indexation will remove one important source of uncertainty in investment planning, the distortion of tax burdens, and this in itself should encourage capital formation.

There is no reason, moreover, why indexing provisions along the lines proposed by the Treasury could not be grafted on to the Bradley-Gephardt proposal or substituted for the flawed indexing rules in the Kemp-Kasten proposal.

Corporation Income

Income originating within corporations (corporate-source income) is now taxed twice—once at the business entity level and a second time when the income is realized by shareholders either as dividends or as capital gains from sale of appreciated stocks. The result: income earned by corporations is taxed more heavily than income earned by unincor-porated businesses, which is taxed only at the personal level. Virtually all our major trading partners have integrated their personal and corpo-ration taxes to a degree. Some proposals give individuals credits for part or all of the taxes paid by corporations; others give corporations deductions for dividends paid, so that interest and dividends are treated alike.[18]

None of the base-broadening proposals examined in this chapter deals adequately with corporate-source income. Again, however, the Treasury plan, which permits corporations to deduct half of dividend payments to individuals, is superior to Bradley-Gephardt and Kemp-Kasten.

Treasury's plan would reduce by more than one-third the degree to which dividends are taxed more heavily than profits of unincorporated businesses.[19] It would do nothing to alleviate any extra burden on

It is logically possible for these two kinds of risks to offset one another and for the overall risk to be less than the parts. But in fact, real economic returns have been low during recent periods of high inflation.

18. For a general discussion of these options, see Charles E. McLure, Jr., *Must Corporate Income Be Taxed Twice?* (Brookings, 1979).

19. Under the Treasury proposal, the top individual rate is 35 percent. If these taxes were fully integrated, corporate source income would be taxed only to individuals at a top rate of 35 percent. Without the dividend deduction, the rate would be 56 percent if all after tax income were distributed $[0.33 + 0.35(0.67) = 0.5645]$. With a 50 percent dividend deduction, corporations pay just under 20 percent of profits in tax if they distribute all net earnings as dividends. In that event, they can distribute just over 80

retained earnings. While it represents a step forward, a margin of double taxation on corporate-source income is inevitable so long as separate and unintegrated income taxes are imposed on corporations and individuals. Again, with appropriate modifications in other elements of their plans, specifically corporate tax rates, such a deduction could be added to the two congressional plans.

Saving and Investment

As explained in chapter 2, an *efficient* tax system would not distort choices between consumption and saving (that is, between current and future consumption); an *equitable* tax system would not impose higher tax burdens on individuals who chose to spend their lifetime resources later in life rather than earlier. On both these counts the current income tax and all three proposals examined in this chapter are inefficient and inequitable. The income tax reduces the future consumption that can be financed out of current earnings by a far larger proportion than it reduces the current consumption that can be financed from the same earnings (see table 2-1). The result is a distortion of saving decisions and discrimination against those who choose to defer consumption.

Piecemeal attempts to deal with these defects of the current income tax create their own problems. For example, tax sheltered saving through qualified pension plans, IRAs, and Keogh plans permits most people to avoid this distortion on most of their savings. As noted in chapter 2, however, these provisions can be used to avoid tax even if no saving occurs. One need merely shift assets into such accounts or borrow to make deposits into them. Thus, the expansion of IRA limits in the Treasury proposal increases opportunities for tax avoidance. Although the Treasury proposal distorts saving, it is neutral across investment decisions. Investment neutrality would forestall the large economic losses now incurred because high-productivity investments often lose out to low-productivity investments that yield higher after-tax returns because of tax preferences. Investment neutrality is a strong point in favor of the Treasury proposal.

Kemp-Kasten, in contrast, distorts the allocation of capital by treating investments in depreciable assets much more favorably than it treats

---

percent of earnings in dividends. With distribution of 80 percent of before-tax profits the combined tax rate is 48 percent $[0.2 + 0.35(0.8) = 0.48]$. The difference between 48 and 56, or 8 percent, is 38 percent of the difference between 56 and 35, or 21 percent.

nondepreciable investments, such as those in inventories, land, and working capital. It thereby penalizes firms and industries that make relatively heavy use of highly taxed assets. Furthermore, Kemp-Kasten continues to allow full deductibility of interest on funds used to finance investments that can be expensed. Such inconsistent treatment of borrowing and investing not only would greatly enlarge the benefits to depreciable capital, but also would allow many individual taxpayers to completely shelter income from taxation.

No annual income tax can avoid the tension between taxing income comprehensively and providing saving and investment opportunities that are unencumbered by the income tax. Reduction of the extra burdens placed on saving and investment inevitably leads to opportunities for tax avoidance by asset shifting or borrowing. All three plans illustrate the dilemma and the tradeoffs.

Summary

The income tax is currently in such sad shape that major improvements can be made simply by removing its existing abnormalities and excesses. By pruning deductions, credits, exclusions, and allowances that have narrowed the tax base, it is possible to simplify the returns of millions of taxpayers, lower marginal rates, and curb incentives that reduce economic efficiency. The Treasury proposal for accomplishing such base-broadening while also measuring real economic income would represent a milestone in tax reform. Although it is more modest in scope, the Bradley-Gephardt proposal also qualifies as a major step forward. The Kemp-Kasten proposal requires more extensive surgery regarding the treatment of capital income. Elements of each plan could be selected for a compromise proposal. Any such plan, however, that remained within the framework of an annual tax on realized income would be unable to correct important flaws in our current tax system. But these problems can be solved if we take an approach to taxation along the lines described in the next chapter.

CHAPTER FOUR

The Cash Flow Income Tax

THE CASH FLOW income tax is based on the principle that all income should be taxed once in the course of a taxpayer's lifetime.[1] As noted in chapter 2, income equals earnings from labor plus earnings on accumulated wealth or, equivalently, it equals consumption plus additions to net worth. The cash flow income tax described in this chapter is imposed on all consumption plus transfers to others through gifts or bequests; it is, therefore, an income tax imposed on resources available to the taxpayer over his or her lifetime. Although it is an income tax, it is free of the distortions that plague the annual income tax. As we will show, it handles realizations and accruals correctly; inflation does not distort its tax base; it is neutral between current and future consumption; and integration of the cash flow income taxes for individuals and corporations is natural and automatic.

1. An earlier version of this plan appeared as chap. 5, "Reforming the Tax System," Alice M. Rivlin, ed., *Economic Choices 1984* (Brookings, 1984). The interested reader may also wish to consult the following sources: William D. Andrews, "A Consumption-Type or Cash Flow Personal Income Tax," *Harvard Law Review*, vol. 87 (April 1974), pp. 1113–88; Anthony B. Atkinson and Joseph E. Stiglitz, *Lectures on Public Economics* (McGraw-Hill, 1980), especially chap. 3; David F. Bradford, "The Economics of Tax Policy Toward Savings," in George M. von Furstenberg, ed., *The Government and Capital Formation* (Ballinger, 1980); David F. Bradford, "Issues in the Design of Savings and Investment Incentives," in Charles R. Hulten, ed., *Depreciation, Inflation, and the Taxation of Income from Capital* (Washington, D.C.: Urban Institute, 1981), pp. 13–47; Robert E. Hall and Alvin Rabushka, *Low Tax, Simple Tax, Flat Tax* (McGraw-Hill, 1983); Sven-Olof Lodin, *Progressive Expenditure Tax—An Alternative?* report of the 1972 Government Commission on Taxation (Stockholm: LiberFörlag, 1978); *The Structure and Reform of Direct Taxation*, report of a committee chaired by J. E. Meade, for the Institute of Fiscal Studies (London: George Allen and Unwin, 1978); Peter Mieszkowski, "The Advisability and Feasibility of an Expenditure Tax System," in Henry J. Aaron and Michael J. Boskin, eds., *The Economics of Taxation* (Brookings, 1980); Joseph A. Pechman, ed., *What Should Be Taxed: Income or Expenditure?* (Brookings, 1980); U.S. Department of the Treasury, *Blueprints for Basic Tax Reform* (Government Printing Office, 1977).

The cash flow income tax would be implemented through incremental changes in the existing personal and corporation income taxes. This chapter describes how each element of the tax would work after the transition is complete. It explains how the tax would improve fairness, efficiency, and ease administration when fully in place. It also shows that the transition to a cash flow income tax would entail no compliance or enforcement problems more serious than those now encountered under the annual income tax.

The Tax on Individuals

The base of the cash flow income tax is cash receipts less cash saving.[2] Under the plan, the tax on income that is saved is deferred until the savings are consumed or transferred to others by gift or bequest. End-of-lifetime wealth, representing unexercised potential consumption of the taxpayer, is included in the tax base of the final tax return. The inclusion of most such transfers is essential to the cash flow income tax. If bequests and gifts were taxed as lightly under the cash flow tax as they are under the current estate and gift taxes, a cash flow base would measure only consumption instead of income.[3]

Receipts include all wages and salaries, rent, interest, profits, dividends, and transfer payments. Cash saving is defined as all payments into certain "qualified accounts," including all financial assets (stocks, bonds, and other securities), all accounts in banks and other depository institutions, and purchase of real estate (except owner-occupied housing). Qualified accounts are defined by the fact that deposits into them are deductible and withdrawals from them are taxable. Gifts received and inheritances are not taxed if they are saved but only when they are consumed or transferred to others. Since dissaving can also take the

2. This plan recognizes that not all inflows of resources to individuals occur in cash form. Income in kind, particularly employer-purchased fringe benefits, is an important source of household income. These benefits can be taxed to the individual or to the employer, as will be explained more fully below.

3. Chap. 2 discusses why consumption is an inferior index of ability to pay. Once wealth transfers are included in the cash flow tax, thereby making it an income tax, the question of whether an additional tax should be levied on bequests, gifts, or even wealth in general hinges on considerations unrelated to income taxation.

form of borrowing, the proceeds of loans are included in the tax base, and loan repayments, including both principal and interest, are deductible in reaching the tax base.[4]

All purchases of depreciable assets are immediately and fully deductible. This rule brings important simplifications in business taxation. Because the cost of capital is fully recovered for tax purposes at time of purchase, there is no need to measure depreciation. Similarly, there is no need to calculate capital gains, because the cost of assets generating these gains would be deducted when purchased. As a result, such assets carry a zero basis, and the proceeds from sales are accordingly taxable in full unless the proceeds are reinvested. The inconsistency between accrued and realized gain, which plays such havoc with the fairness and efficiency of the annual income tax, disappears under the cash flow income tax because accrued gains add equally to income and saving. Cash actually received, net of payments into qualified accounts, would constitute the tax base.

Gifts and bequests to anyone other than one's spouse are treated as consumption when they occur, subject to an averaging provision if the amounts transferred are large. Wealth transfers between spouses at any time are tax free. This set of rules assures that income is taxed once and only once in a generation.

It is desirable to permit each person to make some additional personal gifts or bequests free of tax.[5] For example, moderate transfers between parents or children at time of need and other modest intrafamily gifts or bequests should not be made into taxable events. Sizeable exemptions are undesirable, because they would result in unequal taxes on people with similar lifetime spending capacities. But a lifetime exemption of $100,000 per person ($200,000 per couple) would permit most families to exclude all gifts and bequests from tax without materially eroding the principle that total spending capacity should be taxed in full; most wealth transferred between generations is concentrated in estates larger than these limits.[6]

4. For an exception to this general rule, see the section on special borrowing and averaging provisions in appendix A of this chapter.

5. Charitable contributions are a separate issue and are discussed later in the chapter.

6. Widows and widowers would inherit any unused exemption of their deceased spouse, but no person would be allowed more than a $200,000 exemption, even if successive spouses have died.

Table 4-1. *Tax-Free Levels of Expenditure under Proposed
Cash Flow Income Tax, 1986*
Dollars

Household size and composition	Tax-free levels of expenditure
Single	5,500
Couple, no children	9,000
Couple, one child	11,534[a]
Couple, two children	12,300

a. Includes earned income tax credit of current law indexed to 1986. Without credit, tax-free expenditure is $10,650.

Personal Exemptions

Under the cash flow income tax, larger personal exemptions are allowed than under the present income tax. Our standard is that tax should not be imposed on individuals or families whose consumption is below current poverty thresholds.[7] Based on estimates for 1986, tax-free levels of consumption would be set at $5,500 for a single person, $9,000 for couples, and $1,650 for each additional dependent (table 4-1).

Rates

Tax rates under the cash flow income tax could be set to distribute burdens either more or less progressively than those under current law. For reasons set forth in chapter 1, we present rates that would approximate the current distribution of tax burdens by economic classes. To match current revenues, annual consumption would be taxed as shown in table 4-2: for joint returns, 5 percent tax on the first $11,000 of cash flow in excess of tax-free levels, 20 percent on the next $32,750, and 32 percent on all amounts greater than $43,750. For single taxpayers, the same rates would apply, but the three cash flow brackets would be as follows: less than $5,500; $5,500 to $43,750; and greater than $43,750. These rates and brackets preserve current tax burdens.

7. We recognize that the consistency of the official poverty thresholds has been criticized and that the thresholds for families of different sizes may require revision. For that reason the numbers in the text are illustrative only.

Table 4-2. *Cash Flow Income Tax Rates That Yield the Same Revenue as Current Law, 1986*

Tax rate (percent)	Cash flow brackets[a] (dollars)	
	Single return	Joint return
5	0– 5,500	0–11,000
20	5,500–43,750	11,000–43,750
32	More than 43,750	More than 43,750

a. Cash flow amounts in excess of tax-free amounts shown in table 4-1.

Special Credits and Deductions

Most special credits and deductions should be repealed for the reasons set forth in chapter 2. Most are poorly designed to achieve nonrevenue objectives, and they foster inequity, inefficiency, and complexity. But some provisions, perhaps in modified form, should be retained because they are deeply entrenched or advance important objectives that cannot be promoted in other ways.

TWO-EARNER FAMILIES. If married couples are taxed as a single unit and tax rates are graduated, then marriage must either increase or decrease tax liabilities for some couples.[8] Current law imposes heavier taxes on two earners with similar earnings if they are married than if they are single (the "marriage penalty"). The magnitude of this problem depends on the spread of nominal tax rates (11 percent to 50 percent under current law). To reduce this problem, current law allows a deduction for 10 percent of the earnings of the lesser-earning spouse up to a maximun deduction of $3,000. Because the cash flow income tax and the reform plans examined in chapter 3 reduce the range of marginal rates, the size of the marriage penalty for two-earner couples would be smaller under these plans than under current law. For that reason, the deduction for two-earner couples could be scaled back without aggravating the marriage penalty. Whether some form of the deduction (or perhaps a credit) should be retained depends on social judgments about the importance of eliminating the marriage penalty. In making this

8. No tax system can simultaneously satisfy the following three conditions: that couples with equal income pay equal tax; that tax rates are progressive; and that the tax system treat two people the same whether they are married or not. See Harvey E. Brazer, "Income Tax Treatment of the Family," and Alicia Munnell, "The Couple versus the Individual under the Federal Personal Income Tax," in Henry J. Aaron and Michael J. Boskin, eds., *The Economics of Taxation* (Brookings, 1980), pp. 223–46 and 247–78.

decision, one should keep in mind that steps to reduce the marriage penalty for two-earner couples with similar earnings generally increase a marriage "bonus" for one-earner couples and for two-earner couples where the earnings are dissimilar.

OFFSET TO PAYROLL TAXES. Low earners are now eligible for the earned-income tax credit, which was originally enacted to offset social security payroll taxes. A similar provision should be retained under the cash flow income tax to forestall increased taxes on low-wage workers who now qualify for the credit.

ITEMIZED DEDUCTIONS. Among the activities supported through item-ized deductions, two deserve special mention: charitable giving and homeownership. Charitable organizations play an important part in American life. Evidence strongly suggests that contributions to them would drop sharply if such donations were no longer tax deductible.[9] Because the encouragement to giving is related to the taxpayer's marginal tax rate, any tax reform that leads to lower marginal rates would tend to reduce charitable giving.

It is inequitable for the tax law to provide greater encouragement to giving by high-bracket than by low-bracket taxpayers. Accordingly, we would replace the deduction for charitable giving with a credit based on the maximum marginal tax rate. To ease compliance and enforcement we propose that the credit be limited to gifts exceeding a certain threshold, say the greater of 1 percent of the cash flow income tax base or $100.[10]

The current tax law strongly encourages homeownership. The de-ductibility of mortgage interest and property taxes and the exclusion from tax of capital gains on home sales save taxpayers $37 billion each year.[11] If these subsidies are to be reduced or eliminated, transition rules

9. For a good survey of this literature, see Charles T. Clotfelter and C. Eugene Steuerle, "Charitable Contributions," in Henry J. Aaron and Joseph A. Pechman, eds., *How Taxes Affect Economic Behavior* (Brookings, 1981), pp. 403–46.

10. Gifts of cash or of property for which the donor had not received a deduction at time of purchase would be subject to the credit. The credit for gifts in kind would be based on the market value of such property. Gifts of financial assets or any other asset that is treated as a qualified account would not be eligible for the credit. The taxpayer received a deduction when such assets were acquired and would have to pay tax when they were sold to finance consumption or when they were transferred to others by gift or bequest. The incentive to give property held in qualified accounts comes from the fact that the taxpayer will be spared such tax by making the charitable contribution.

11. This estimate compares actual revenues with those that would result if these tax

are necessary to avoid shocks to housing markets and to homeowners. This important issue is examined at greater length below.

All other personal deductions or credits would be severely limited. Deductions for health expenses and casualty losses (not covered by insurance) in excess of 10 percent of income should be retained because both represent an involuntary use of wealth. The cost of employer-purchased health insurance and any other consumption goods provided by employers should be treated as taxable consumption by covered employees. Where imputation to employees is impossible, deductions for the cost of such goods should be denied to employers.

How the Cash Flow Income Tax Would Work

Most taxpayers would find the tax return under the cash flow income tax similar to the current return; the rest would find it much simpler. Taxpayers would list all earnings, as they do under the current income tax, as well as net receipts from, or payments into, qualified accounts. Documentation supporting these transactions would be similar to W-2 forms now used to support reported earnings. Taxpayers with numerous transactions in qualified accounts could reduce the number of such required forms by maintaining a single cash management account through which all transactions in qualified accounts were handled. In that event, the single form for the cash management account would summarize all such transactions. Few taxpayers would have sufficient medical expenses or casualty losses to justify separate reporting of these items. Starting with cash flow from earnings, they would add net withdrawals from qualified accounts (or subtract net deposits) to reach taxable income, to which they would apply the three rate brackets to calculate their tax. They would then subtract any available credits.

Here's how the cash flow income tax would work for one year in a simple but plausible hypothetical case. John and Mary Dean each earn $20,000 and live in a rented apartment. Their uninsured medical expenses and casualty losses for the year were less than 10 percent of cash flow. They deposited $5,000 in a savings account and sold $2,000 of stock purchased in a previous year. They donated $200 to charity. Their return would fit easily on one page, as indicated in table 4-3.

---

benefits to owner-occupied housing were not available. *Special Analyses, Budget of the United States Government, FY 1985* (GPO, 1984), pp. G-44–G-45.

Table 4-3. *Hypothetical Tax Return of John and Mary Dean*
Dollars

Item	Amount
Cash flow	
1a. Wages and salaries	40,000
b. Other earnings	0
c. Total earnings	40,000
2a. Withdrawals from qualified accounts	2,000
b. Deposits in qualified accounts	5,000
3. Cash flow (line 1c plus 2a less 2b)	37,000
4. Deduction for medical expenses and casualty losses (excess over 10 percent of line 3)	0
5. Exemption for tax-free cash flow (see table 4-1)	9,000
6. Taxable cash flow (line 3 less lines 4 and 5)	28,000
7. Tax (see table 4-2)	3,950
Credits	
8a. Charitable contributions credit	0
b. Earned-income credit	0
c. Other credits (if any)	0
d. Sum of lines 8a, 8b, and 8c	0
Tax due (line 7 less line 8d)	3,950

Their tax base would be $28,000 calculated as follows: their earnings, $40,000; less their net additions to qualified accounts of $3,000 (their deposit into a savings account of $5,000, less their sale of stock of $2,000); less $9,000 (the tax-exempt cash flow for a couple filing jointly). They would not be eligible for the earned income credit (because their earnings are too high) or for a charitable contributions credit (because their contributions were less than 1 percent of cash flow). Their tax would be 5 percent of $11,000 (or $550) plus 20 percent of $17,000 (or $3,400) for a total of $3,950. During the year they would be subject to withholding tax on their earnings, as under current law.[12]

Under current law, the Deans would pay $4,975 in income taxes in 1986. The substantial reduction in their tax liability is a result of the relatively few tax preferences they claim. Taxpayers who make heavy use of the itemized deductions, credits, and exclusions would pay more tax than they do under current law.

12. The amount withheld would be based on assumptions regarding cash flow from all sources. As under current law, taxpayers whose cash flow was expected to differ significantly from earnings would be able to adjust the amounts withheld or make quarterly estimated payments. No major change in withholding arrangements would be necessary.

Additional complications could arise if the couple had business income, if they were entitled to the special tax advantages for homeowners described below, if medical expenses or casualty losses exceeded 10 percent of cash flow, or if the couple had asset transactions that could not be handled through a cash management account.

Special Problems

Any tax system must resolve a host of technical issues. Several major issues are examined briefly in this section and in greater detail in appendix A to this chapter. Because of the technical nature of this section, it can be skipped without loss of continuity. The technical issues addressed here can be expressed as a series of questions:

What special rules are required for large variations in cash flow?

How should investment in owner-occupied housing be handled?

How should expenditures on post-secondary education be treated?

What steps should be taken to assure that the taxation of wealth transfers is effective?

How should international migration and multinational corporations be handled?

Since many states have income taxes that use items from the current federal income tax, what problems of coordination are likely to arise and how can they be solved?

To avoid double taxation in the transition from the old tax rules to the new, what should be the treatment of consumption and wealth transfers that occur after the change in tax law but that are financed with assets that were acquired before the change (and hence that have already been taxed)?

Special Borrowing and Averaging Provisions

Two provisions would spare most taxpayers additional burdens when they make large outlays. First, each family would be permitted to have outstanding loans of up to $20,000 ($10,000 for single returns) without having to add the proceeds to current income. This provision would permit households to borrow—for example, to finance the purchase of a car or household furnishings—without incurring an extra current tax liability. Repayments of principle and interest would not be deductible, however, if households excluded the proceeds of the loan from cash flow. This option places special administrative responsibilities on financial institutions to ensure that this limit is not exceeded, a point we expand below. Second, to prevent the transfers from being taxed entirely at the maximum marginal rate, a special ten-year averaging provision would be available to taxpayers making gifts or bequests.

Housing

As noted earlier, investments in owner-occupied housing are taxed more favorably under current law than they would be under a true annual income tax, a consumed income tax, or a cash flow income tax. Current law allows homeowners to deduct mortgage interest and property taxes, two major expenses associated with homeownership, but does not require that any of the value of rental services be reported as income. Two issues must be resolved in the taxation of investments in owner-occupied housing. What should be the rules for taxing owner-occupied housing under a cash flow income tax if it is to be treated like other investment? And to what extent should housing be accorded preferential treatment?

The neutral taxation of investments in owner-occupied housing is complicated by the fact that the "yield" on these investments, imputed net rent, is an in-kind benefit and not actual cash flow. Nonetheless, neutral rules for housing can be developed and are presented in appendix A to this chapter.

The more salient question is whether current concessions to homeownership should be retained. Rules that would treat housing like other investments impose higher taxes on homeowners than does current law. While such a shift would be logical tax policy and might be desirable long-run investment policy, it would impose hardships on many homeowners and would abandon a longstanding commitment to promote homeownership.

Accordingly, any reformed tax system is likely to include special provisions to encourage homeownership. One approach, to retain part or all of the current deductions for mortgage interest and property taxes, has an important disadvantage in that it provides greatest assistance to people in the highest tax brackets, who least need assistance in becoming or remaining homeowners. Alternatively, taxpayers might be given a credit based on mortgage interest and property taxes; a credit would provide the same incentive to all taxpayers, regardless of which tax rate they faced.[13]

New incentives to homeownership might be introduced for first-time homebuyers. Other concessions to homeowners can be designed that protect most existing homeowners from large or immediate losses while reducing, if not removing, distortions and inequities in the tax code. We suggest that the goals of any provisions to promote homeownership should be to limit the loss of home values for existing owners and to provide continuing encouragement for home purchase by households with low or moderate income. In no case, however, would it be desirable to protect homeowners fully from the reductions in the value of preferences occasioned by reduced tax rates.

Capital Gains

Because investors would be entitled to deduct the full cost of most assets at time of purchase and would be required to include in taxable income the full proceeds from asset sales (unless reinvested), there would be no need under the cash flow income tax to calculate capital gains on most assets. Such consumer goods as works of art and jewelry, which are commonly bought in part for expected appreciation in value, are a significant exception to this rule. Because their purchase price would not be deductible, only appreciation should be taxed (after adjusting for inflation) when these assets are sold. Households would therefore be required to report as income the difference between the cost of such assets as jewelry or works of art and the proceeds from sale. This rule simply continues current law with the addition of indexing.

Post-secondary Education and Training

Expenditures on post-secondary education and training, including private colleges and universities and vocational training, frequently cause large bulges in household outlays. Although a case can be made for treating such outlays as deductible investments instead of consump-

13. The distinction between deductions and credits is sometimes unclear. The Bradley-Gephardt proposal, described in chap. 3, would permit a deduction for mortgage interest and property taxes, but only against the first bracket rate of 14 percent. As a result, the deduction would reduce taxes by 14 percent of these payments for all homeowners, exactly as a 14 percent credit would do.

tion, this approach would create serious difficulties and is not part of our plan, for reasons set forth in the appendix. Instead, the additional taxes that such outlays would otherwise cause can be deferred by allowing parents or children to average college outlays over several years or by permitting them to exclude the proceeds of college loans from current taxable income. If the latter approach were taken, deductions for repayments of principle and interest would also be denied. The same approach could be applied to vocational education or training.

It should be emphasized here however, that the greatest encouragement to higher education, housing, and other large personal expenditures under the cash flow income tax would be the opportunity to accumulate savings without tax until the funds are spent. A person in the 32 percent bracket who wished to save for a child's college education eighteen years in the future and who could invest at 12 percent would have to earn and set aside 47 percent less under the cash flow income tax than under the current annual income tax.

Gifts, Bequests, and Trusts

The taxation of gifts, bequests, and assets transferred into trusts is an essential element of the cash flow income tax. The various techniques commonly used to avoid the existing estate and gift taxes would have to be curbed. In most cases the taxable amount would be the value of the asset transferred (exceptions are examined in the appendix). The rules would be the same whether the asset were transferred during the donor's life (as a gift) or after the donor's death (as a bequest). Appendix A describes how trusts should be taxed under the cash flow income tax, including the special problems when the creator of a trust retains some ownership rights. It also describes how to discourage the use of generation-skipping trusts to avoid taxes.

International Migration

Without special rules, the cash flow income tax would permit individuals to consume income free of tax by moving wealth out of the country and spending it abroad. This tax avoidance would be prevented by treating the movement of wealth out of the United States as a taxable event. Consistent with this rule, deductions for saving would be allowed only for deposits at institutions located in the United States and subject to U.S. regulations. Also, to deal with individuals who could leave their wealth in the United States but draw down these asset holdings to sustain consumption abroad, a withholding tax should be imposed on all payments from U.S. accounts to persons or businesses not resident in the United States. These provisions would remove any tax incentive to emigrate. For symmetrical reasons, immigrants should be permitted to bring assets into the United States and to consume them without tax, just as they can under current law.

State Income Tax

The introduction of the cash flow income tax would create strong incentives for states to revise their personal and corporation income taxes to take advantage of the simplified filing procedures available under the new system. Otherwise, taxpayers would be required to maintain records and make calculations for the state tax that are unnecessary under the cash flow system.

Transition

Taxpayers who have saved under the current tax rules and then draw down their assets under the cash flow system to finance consumption would, in the absence of transition rules, be taxed twice—first when they save under the old annual income tax and second when they spend under the new cash flow income tax. To prevent such inequities, we recommend rules to permit the tax-free consumption or transfer of assets bought with income that was taxed before the law changed.

Generally speaking, these transition rules should permit taxpayers to recover free of tax the "adjusted basis" of assets held at adoption of the cash flow income tax. For example, consider a person who bought stock for $10,000 under the old system and sells it under the new system; under the transition rules, up to $10,000 of any proceeds from the sale would be tax free. Additional adjustments and restrictions, described in appendix A, would be necessary to assure that this provision worked smoothly; but none would require any records other than those now maintained for payment of capital gains taxes. The transition would take many years to complete; but once all assets acquired before adoption of the cash flow income tax had been sold or transferred to others by gift or bequest, taxpayers would generally not need to maintain any tax records of asset purchase prices.

Business Taxation

Scrapping the corporation income tax altogether and taxing corporate-source income only when it is paid out to individuals has some appeal. Since 1951 the proportion of federal revenue dereived from the corporation income tax has gradually declined, from 32 percent of federal revenue in 1952 to 23 percent in 1960, 17 percent in 1970, and an estimated 9 percent in 1985.[14]

Unfortunately, scrapping the corporation income tax would raise three serious problems. First, the rapidly growing flow to foreign investors of U.S. corporate-source income would escape taxation. Second, owners of corporations would be able to use their businesses to avoid personal taxes by having corporations buy consumption goods for them such as automobiles, housing, life insurance, health care, or legal services—indeed, almost anything.[15] Third, there would be a windfall gain for current corporate owners of depreciable capital. For these reasons a corporation tax should be retained.

The cash flow income tax to be paid by business has two parts: a tax on cash flow to individuals and a withholding tax on payments to foreign investors and corporations.

The corporation tax base would comprise receipts from all sources, including borrowing but excluding proceeds from the sale of stock, less all expenses including capital investments when paid for. Cash flow generated by unincorporated businesses would be similarly calculated, but it would be attributed directly to the owners of the business, as under current law, rather than taxed separately at the level of the business entity. Deductions for business expenditures on consumption items purchased for the benefit of employees or owners would be denied unless

14. *Historical Tables of the Budget of the United States Government, Fiscal Year 1986,* table 2.1.

15. This problem exists under current law as well because such expenditures on behalf of owners are in reality a distribution of income from the corporation to a shareholder and should be taxable as such both to the corporation and to the shareholder. The problem could be handled under the cash flow income tax by treating such expenditures as consumption or as nondeductible business expenses, although valuation questions would certainly arise much as they do under current law.

these outlays were imputed to individuals and included in their taxable receipts.

The second levy on businesses would be a withholding tax on all dividends, interest, rents, and royalties they pay to foreign investors and corporations. This tax would be equivalent to the current withholding taxes on payments abroad and could be credited against other taxes due in the foreign country. Taxation of international businesses is among the most complicated elements of most tax systems. The rules under the cash-flow income tax would not be as complex as current law, but they would not be simple.

Taxing Business Cash Flow to U.S. Residents

The corporate tax base would include the proceeds from borrowing, and all debt service payments would be deductible. If firms borrowed to finance investment, no tax would be imposed in the year the investment was made, because the expenditure on the investment would just offset the proceeds from the loan. If earnings on the investment in subsequent periods differed from the deductible repayment of debt, corporate cash flow and tax liabilities would be affected at those times. Consistent with the nondeductibility of stock issues, no deductions would be permitted for dividend payments or any other cash distribution to shareholders. Purchases of stock by one corporation in another would not be deductible, nor would corporations be taxed on dividends they receive from other corporations. Therefore, if a corporation paid out such dividends to its own shareholders, its tax liabilities would be unaffected.

Similar principles would be applied to cash flow of unincorporated businesses. In particular, new investments would be immediately deductible, and borrowing would be taxable, but the effects would be registered directly in the tax bases of the owners. Owners of unincorporated businesses could offset tax on any positive net cash flow by reinvesting the proceeds within the business or elsewhere.

THE INTEGRATION OF CORPORATE AND INDIVIDUAL TAXES. Although a separate cash flow tax is paid by corporations and not by unincorporated businesses, consistent application of cash flow accounting automatically integrates corporate and individual taxes. As a result, an investor receives the same after-tax return whether investing in a corporation or in an unincorporated business. The following example illustrates this important point.

Table 4-4. *Investment in Unincorporated and Incorporated Business under the Cash Flow Income Tax*[a]
Dollars unless otherwise specified

Item	Unincorporated business	Incorporated business
1. Saving and investment by individual	10,000	10,000
2. After-tax cost to individual	6,800	6,800
3. Funds received by business	10,000	10,000
4. Assets purchased by business	10,000	14,925
5. Business cash flow (at 20% return)	2,000	2,985
6. Business tax	. . .	985
7. Cash flow to individual	2,000	2,000
8. Individual tax	640	640
9. Net after-tax cash flow to individual	1,360	1,360
10. Rate of return to individual (percent) (line 9 ÷ line 2)	20	20

a. Assumes a 32 percent individual tax rate, a 33 percent corporate tax rate, and a 20 percent cash flow return on business investment.

Consider an investor in the 32 percent marginal tax bracket who is contemplating investing $10,000 in either an unincorporated enterprise, say a partnership, or in a corporation subject to a 33 percent tax rate.[16] In each case, the business earns 20 percent before tax on funds invested and pays all after-tax cash flow to the investor. The relevant cash flows and taxes are shown in table 4-4. In the first column, the partnership case, the individual invests $10,000 in the partnership, which uses these funds to buy income-producing property. The investor's tax bill is thereby reduced by 32 percent of this amount, or $3,200, and the investor's net after-tax cost of transferring $10,000 in property to the business is therefore $6,800. The business earns 20 percent on the investment and pays out this sum, $2,000, to the individual investor. The investor then pays $640 in tax on this flow for a net return of $1,360, equal to 20 percent of the net (after-tax) investment of $6,800.

If the individual invests in a corporation rather than a partnership, the corporation receives the $10,000 and the investor again has an after-tax investment of $6,800. The corporation can buy $14,925 worth of property with the $10,000 proceeds, because it can immediately deduct $14,925 and, given its 33 percent marginal tax rate, realize a tax savings of $4,925.

16. These rates are, respectively, the top individual tax rate and the corporation tax rate under the cash flow income tax. Appendix B of this chapter shows that a 33 percent tax rate on corporate cash flow matches the current revenue yield of the corporation income tax.

The net cost of $10,000 to the firm is the amount received from the individual shareholder. These assets of $14,925 then earn a 20 percent return, or $2,985 in cash flow. If the corporation pays out all proceeds, it incurs a tax liability equal to 33 percent of $2,985. Thus, it pays $985 in taxes and $2,000 to the investor, who again must pay $640 in tax and ends up with an after-tax cash flow of $1,360, or 20 percent of the net investment, exactly the same position as in the partnership case.

The separate corporate cash flow tax on earnings paid to investors does not, therefore, change the rate of return to the corporation or to the individual shareholder. The tax exactly offsets the advantage of immediate deductibility of the cost of acquiring assets. The result is perfect integration of corporate and individual cash flows with no distortions imposed by the corporate tax.

EXPENSING AS GOVERNMENT INVESTMENT. The full, immediate deduction of new investment, or "expensing," in effect makes the government a partner with the private invester. When a business deducts the cost of investment from its tax base, the government shares in the cost of the investments. If the business deduction lowers the governments tax revenues by $1,000, the government can be represented as borrowing $1,000 to counterbalance the revenue loss. The government recovers its "investment" by collecting tax on the cash flow generated by the investment. The government comes out even when the flow of such taxes, discounted at the government's borrowing rate, just equals the initial revenue loss. The government makes a "profit" when the discounted flow of taxes is greater than the government's borrowing rate, a "loss" when it is less.

Part of the return earned by the corporation in excess of the government's borrowing rate represents profits enjoyed by firms with particularly favorable market positions. Taxation of "rents" on these advantages contributes to the overall efficiency of the tax system relative to a tax system that leaves such rents untaxed. Part of the return above the government's borrowing rate represents compensation for the riskiness of some corporate investments or for the entrepreneurship associated with such investments. But as the example in table 4-4 illustrates, because the government is a partner in the business, the cash flow income tax does not reduce the rate of return that individuals receive on their own after-tax contribution to the business enterprise.

Immediate deduction or expensing of the cost of investment would generate negative cash flow for new firms with high start-up costs or for any other firm undertaking large, equity-financed investments relative to current cash receipts. For deductibility to be as valuable on investments undertaken by such firms as it would be for firms with positive cash flow, some additional steps must be taken. Firms could be provided rebates for deductions causing a negative cash flow. This procedure would mean that new firms without current profits would benefit currently from the deductions, just as would older firms with profits against which deductions could be offset. However, this approach suffers from an important disadvantage; to prevent abuse, the tax authorities would have to distinguish between regular business investment and hobby investments, such as weekend farms or special companies created to invest in art that is then enjoyed by the owner.

Alternatively, firms could be allowed to carry tax losses forward to be applied against future cash flow. If this course were followed, the losses should be accumulated with interest to prevent their erosion in present-value terms—a potentially serious problem when interest rates are high. Firms could also be allowed to offset any current negative cash flow against previous positive cash flow and receive rebates of previous taxes paid, similar to net operating loss carrybacks allowed under current law.[17] For new firms, these approaches would not provide the same current cash benefits from investment deductions as would the immediate rebate approach, but they are substantially better than current law since they would maintain the present value of the tax write-off.

Taxing Multinational Corporations

Financial flows between U.S. corporations and their foreign subsidiaries would be treated under the general rules applying to any other investments by a U.S. corporation. Thus, purchases of equity interests in, or loans to, foreign subsidiaries would be deductible, and repatriated dividends and interest would be taxable.[18] Also, no credit would be allowed for foreign taxes paid, but an implicit deduction for foreign taxes

17. In principle, past taxes should also be increased by the discount factor. But as long as interest is paid on loss carry-forwards, the significance of this additional refinement is limited.

18. Purchases of stock by domestic corporations in other domestic corporations would not be deductible, but loans to domestic corporations would be deductible. In the case of contributions of funds to foreign subsidiaries, no distinction would be made between debt and equity; both would be deductible.

is provided since taxable cash dividends received from abroad would be net of foreign taxes paid.

U.S. subsidiaries of foreign corporations would be taxed in the same manner as other U.S. corporations. Both would be permitted to deduct the cost of investments, and both would be taxed on dividends paid to shareholders, including foreign shareowners. In addition, a withholding tax would be imposed on all remittances to foreign shareholders. This withholding tax would be identical to the current withholding tax on payments abroad by U.S.-owned corporations and would represent a tax payment for which a foreign tax credit could be allowed by the foreign country. In other words, a business incorporated in the United States would be treated the same whether majority ownership or control was domestic or foreign.

U.S. corporations and their foreign branches would maintain consolidated accounts for calculating the cash flow income tax. U.S. branches of foreign corporations would continue to pay a tax according to present income tax rules as a proxy for the withholding tax on cash distributions to foreigners by U.S. corporations.

Possible Disadvantages of a Cash Flow Income Tax

The changes in rules under the cash flow income tax would impose some additional administrative burdens if individuals continue to behave exactly as they do now. People could avoid these burdens, however, by changing the way they carry out transactions. Moreover, they would find it optimal to undertake the same investments under the cash flow system as they would in the absence of taxes.

Borrowing

Administrative procedures for handling loans and repayments of interest and principal would have to change under the cash flow system. Because the proceeds of loans would enter the tax base, some borrowers would want to negotiate loans sufficient not only to meet their borrowing needs but also to cover the additional tax generated by the loan. Although the extra borrowing would be an extra burden, the privilege of deducting repayments of principal and interest would offset it. Those who avoid current taxes on borrowing by using the $20,000 exemption proposed earlier would surrender their right to deduct future repayments.

Reporting Requirements

Under current law, deposits and withdrawals from bank accounts do not normally have tax consequences. Under the cash flow income tax, taxpayers would have to report withdrawals and deposits of both principal and interest.

As noted earlier, the burden of monitoring transactions and cash flows into and out of qualified accounts could be virtually eliminated if taxpayers used the equivalent of a cash management account. Such institutions as banks, savings and loan associations, brokerage houses, or other organizations could carry out all transactions into and out of qualified accounts and maintain records for taxpayers. At year's end, the financial institution would send the taxpayer a form listing all such transactions and the net addition to or subtraction from taxable cash flow. With such a statement it would be no more difficult for taxpayers to fill in a tax return and attach the form than it is now to list wages and salaries. It would be no more difficult for institutions to provide the necessary information than it is now for banks to provide monthly checking account statements or end-of-year summaries of payments of interest and principal on home mortgages. These procedures would be simpler than the cumbersome calculations necessary to report stock purchases and sales, real estate transactions, and other capital items. They would be far simpler than the calculations required to calculate inflation-adjusted capital income under the Treasury Department's proposed reforms.

Taxation of Entrepreneurial Income

The cash flow system would tax a small part of entrepreneurial income twice. Business income consists not only of returns on replaceable capital, including structures, equipment, and inventories, but also of returns on entrepreneurial effort. The rate of return on replaceable capital is unaffected by the cash flow income tax, because the investment costs are immediately deducted. But returns to entrepreneurship—the compensation for risk taking and organizational activities—may in some special cases be taxed not only as personal income but also as business cash flow.

Most entrepreneurial income would be taxed only once, at the personal level, as the following three cases indicate. First, where entrepreneurial activity is performed by managers of large corporations, compensation is deductible by the corporation and is taxed only once, at the personal level. Second, where such activity is performed by single proprietors or partners, there is no corporation tax. Third, where entrepreneurs also act as venture capitalists and make tax-deductible contributions of capital to risky corporate ventures, a separate tax is levied on dividends, but as the example in table 4-4 illustrates, the separate tax does not reduce the rate of return on the capital contributed. As long as the entrepreneur acquires shares of stock in the corporation proportional to his or her actual capital contribution, there is no double tax on entrepreneurship. These three cases account for most entrepreneurial activity in the United States.

Double taxation of entrepreneurship can, but need not, occur where an individual receives shares of stock not for capital contributions but as a reward for creative or managerial contributions. In such cases, there is no deduction for a capital investment to offset the corporation tax on dividends paid. As a result, such dividends are fully exposed to both the corporate and personal cash flow taxes.

There would be no double tax even in this situation if entrepreneurs could negotiate large wage payments contingent on business success. Only if such contracts could not be negotiated would entrepreneurial compensation be taxed twice. In that event, the return to entrepreneurship received as dividends or capital gains would be taxed twice, once at the business and once at the personal level, with no offsetting relief provided by tax-deductible capital contributions. Thus, a small portion of entrepreneurial income might be subject to double taxation.

Evasion Incentives

Certain incentives to evade tax would increase under the cash flow income tax. Although transactions in capital goods may generate a taxable gain or loss under the current income tax, the entire sum involved in the transaction is a taxable item under the cash flow income tax. The larger sum produces a greater incentive to conceal asset sales. A person who buys a bond for $9,000 and then sells it for $10,000 under the annual income tax would be required to report the $1,000 gain. Under the cash flow income tax, the same person would have been given a $9,000 deduction but would later be required to report a $10,000 cash flow on his or her tax return. Clearly, the second case creates a much greater incentive than does the first to report the purchase and conceal the sale. This incentive is a key reason to require complete reporting of financial transactions by financial institutions. It would also be desirable to require purchasers of financial assets to report the name of the seller of such assets along with their claims for deductions, thus facilitating cross-checks. In any event, it is clear that auditing of asset transactions would have to increase under a cash flow income tax.

Conclusion

The cash flow income tax, like the reforms of the annual income tax examined in the last chapter, would do away with the distortions, complexity, and inequity arising from numerous special features that clutter current tax law. In addition, however, the cash flow income tax would solve the four fundamental problems that other proposed reforms solve imperfectly, if at all: inflation effects, untaxed accruals, double taxation of corporate income, and the distortion of the choice to consume or save. Here is a recap of these points.

The distortions caused by inflation—the erosion of deductions for capital depreciation, the mismeasurement of capital gains, the misstatement of real interest income and deductions, and the understatement of cost of goods sold—all would disappear. Because all outlays for saving or investment would be fully deductible when they are made, there would be no deferred deductions to be eroded by inflation.

The cash flow income tax eliminates the need to determine when accrued gains are realized, because cash flows alone would count in determining tax liability. A savings account in which interest accrues would be treated exactly like appreciating stock. In both cases, tax would be due only when the asset is liquidated to finance consumption or when it is transferred to others. The amount a person can spend or transfer would be unaffected by the timing of the sale of an asset. Unrealized gains would not enter the tax base.

The cash flow income tax on corporations would be fully integrated with the personal cash flow tax. In contrast to current law, the two taxes would fall with equal weight on corporate and noncorporate investment. Tax-induced distortions favoring partnerships over corporations, debt financing over equity financing within corporations, and retained earnings over dividends would disappear.

The cash flow income tax would virtually eliminate distortion in the timing of consumption. The current tax imposes widely varying tax rates on persons with the same spending opportunities who time consumption differently. In contrast, the present value of tax liabilities under the cash flow income tax is the same whether one consumes income as earned, saves it for later consumption, or transfers it to others.

Nor does the cash flow income tax distort personal decisions about how much to save or in what to invest. Both savers and investors would receive the same return under the cash flow income tax as they would in the absence of taxes. As a result, the personal and corporate cash flow income taxes reduce or eliminate most distortions of saving and investment that would exist under even the most carefully crafted annual income tax. Thus the cash flow system not only meets the test of fairness but terminates tax-induced distortions in saving.

There is some reason to think that adoption of a cash flow income tax would increase household saving. Such an increase would be desirable, but its importance should not be overestimated. The fundamental justification for the cash flow income tax should rest not on its problematic saving effects but on its fairness, its ability to reduce distortions in investment and saving, and its ease of administration.

APPENDIX A: TECHNICAL PROBLEMS

IN THE MAIN TEXT of this chapter we briefly discussed the major technical problems that the cash flow income tax must solve. We examine the solutions in more detail here.

Special Borrowing and Averaging Provisions

Two provisions would help prevent bulges in consumption or asset transfers from pushing taxpayers into higher tax brackets than they would occupy if these outlays were evenly distributed. First, to handle bulges in consumption, all taxpayers would be allowed some general borrowing outside the framework of qualified accounts. We suggest a

$20,000 ceiling for joint returns ($10,000 for single returns) on the amount of such loans that could be outstanding at one time.[19] The proceeds from such loans would not be included in the tax base, and the repayments of principal and interest would not be deductible. Excluding the proceeds of a loan from the tax base spares taxpayers the need to borrow enough for the payment of taxes on the loan proceeds. This arrangement would be especially helpful to young couples making large outlays to establish their households.[20]

A second averaging provision would be available to taxpayers for gifts and bequests. To prevent such items from pushing people into higher brackets than their average cash-flow would justify, taxpayers would have the option of using a special ten-year averaging provision. The taxpayer would calculate the incremental tax on one-tenth of the gift or bequest and pay ten times that amount in tax. A married taxpayer with $20,000 in total cash flow exclusive of gifts or bequests who is in the 20 percent bracket and who gives or bequeaths $100,000 in excess of his lifetime exemption would face a tax of $28,070 on the transfer if there were no averaging.[21] With ten-year averaging, the taxpayer would calculate the incremental tax on one-tenth of the transfer, or $10,000; since all of this amount would be taxed at 20 percent, the incremental tax would be $2,000. Consequently, the total tax of ten times the incremental tax would be only $20,000 rather than $28,070.[22]

Housing

Two-thirds of all American families own their own homes. For the majority the house is their most important marketable asset. Both political and economic reasons dictate that homeowners be fairly treated.

19. Taxpayers would also be allowed to borrow additional sums under the same arrangements to finance tuition for post-secondary education, as explained below.

20. A couple that borrowed the same amount through a qualified account would pay tax on the proceeds from the loan, but they would be entitled to deduct interest and principal as the loan is repaid. Since the present value of the proceeds of a loan, by definition, equals the present value of the loan repayments, these approaches are equivalent.

21. Of the $100,000 transferred, $32,750 would be taxed at 20 percent (because total cash flow of $20,000 for a joint return with no children puts the taxpayer at the bottom of the 20 percent bracket) and $67,250 would be taxed at 32 percent, yielding a total tax on the transfer of $28,070.

22. A similar averaging provision would be available for home purchases or payment for post-secondary education, as described below.

Current Tax Treatment

People who invest in owner-occupied housing may deduct major expenses associated with that investment—mortgage interest and property taxes. But they are not required to report as income any of the rental value of housing services their investment produces. If owner-occupied housing were treated like other investments under the current income tax, homeowners would pay tax on net imputed rent (NR), measured as the excess of estimated gross market rent (GR) over mortgage interest (MI), property taxes (PT), and all other overhead expenses including depreciation (OE). That is, they would pay tax on $NR = GR - PT - MI - OE$. They are already allowed to deduct $MI + PT$. To correctly measure and tax imputed rental income one could either disallow deductions for PT and MI and include NR in the tax base directly, or indirectly calculate NR by introducing deductions for OE and including GR in the tax base.

In other words, investments in owner-occupied housing are now treated more favorably than they would be if the tax system exempted them. Exemption would require disallowance of deductions for mortgage interest and property taxes. To tax housing like other investments, it would be necessary in addition to include in each homeowner's tax base an estimate of imputed net rental income on his or her home equity.

Housing under the Cash Flow Income Tax

If investment in owner-occupied housing were treated like any other investment under the cash flow income tax, the purchase price would be immediately deductible and the withdrawals from qualified accounts or the proceeds from loans used to pay for the house would be included in taxable receipts. These transactions would exactly offset one another in the year of purchase. Repayments of principal and interest on the mortgage loan would be deductible, but imputed rental income from the house would be entered as a taxable receipt. As with any other investment, any difference would be reflected in the tax base.

This method of dealing with owner-occupied housing is technically correct, but like the taxation of gross imputed rent under the income tax, it would raise both practical and political problems. The practical problem is that estimating a market rent for tax purposes would be inexact and open to challenge. But if gross imputed rental receipts are excluded from the tax base, a deduction for loan repayments will perpetuate the large tax shelter owner occupants now enjoy.

Excluding all aspects of the purchase of a home from the tax system would avoid this problem. That is, no deduction would be given for the investment, and neither the proceeds of mortgages nor their repayments would have any effect on tax. Compared to present tax law, this approach amounts to the denial of the mortgage interest deduction.[23] However, the withdrawals from qualified accounts for downpayments, like withdrawals for other purposes, would remain taxable under this approach.

This approach would be the easiest way to treat housing the same as other investments. The one remaining problem—the large bulge in tax resulting from the downpayments—could be dealt with by an averaging rule. That is, each year for perhaps ten years a fraction of the downpayment plus interest—calculated as a level-payment mortgage—could be added to the tax base. Thus, a practical approach to the taxation of owner-occupied housing under the cash flow income tax can be developed.

But such an approach does not deal with the political problem that will arise from reducing tax benefits that are so deeply ingrained and so widely distributed.

Concessions in Housing

Existing tax concessions to housing lower the out-of-pocket cost of homeownership and prop up housing prices.[24] These advantages can be reduced in two ways: by denying deductions or by cutting tax rates. This means that any base-broadening tax reform that permits a reduction in marginal tax rates will lower tax benefits for homeowners. Implementing either the cash flow income tax or the reforms examined in chapter 3 would all lower benefits of homeownership *even if all existing deductions are preserved.*

23. Ideally, the deduction for property taxes would also be denied under this approach.

24. One of the explanations for the rapid rise of house prices during the 1970s was that the interaction of inflation and the treatment of housing under the income tax converted owner-occupancy into a valuable tax shelter. Deductible interest outlays rose with inflation and generated immediate tax savings. The compensating inflation-related increase in house prices was untaxed until the house was sold; and even then the gain was excluded, in whole or in part, from the tax base. See Frank De Leeuw and Larry Ozane, "Housing," in Henry J. Aaron and Joseph A. Pechman, eds., *How Taxes Affect Economic Behavior* (Brookings, 1981), pp. 283–319.

Although basic principles of tax design would call for the complete termination of current home-ownership preferences to eliminate distortions in investment and consumption, such a "cold turkey" approach is unlikely to be politically viable. Nor would it be fair to many homeowners. Because current tax advantages have been capitalized into existing house prices, the withdrawal of these advantages would result in capital losses, a potentially severe problem for many homeowners whose house is their primary store of wealth. In addition, these tax advantages have greatly reduced the costs of home ownership and have induced many homeowners to undertake expenditure obligations they could not otherwise sustain and cannot easily escape.

It would be possible to keep down the out-of-pocket costs of homeowners by grandfathering current tax privileges for existing homeowners or alternatively by preserving the mortgage interest deduction for the life of existing loans. But would-be buyers would not have these advantages available to them and, accordingly, would not be able to pay as much to buy a house. Thus, prices of existing houses would still tend to fall.

Maintaining permanent tax preferences for owner-occupied housing is one way to support home values. If this course is followed, it would be important to decide whether concessions should be restricted to particular groups of actual or potential homeowners, to specific items of housing cost, to maximum dollar amounts, and to one rate of subsidy, or whether the arbitrary rules of current law (described in chapter 2) should apply. Many techniques exist to concentrate the assistance on households who would be least likely to buy a house without special encouragement. As one example, homeowners might be allowed a credit of, say, 20 percent of mortgage interest payments up to some maximum amount, say $6,000 per year (maximum credit of $1,200 per year).

Capital Gains

Sales of used consumer goods would not in general be subject to tax. Because the owner received no deduction when the good was purchased and hence paid full tax on the cost of the good, to impose another tax on the proceeds from sale would be double taxation.

Transactions in some commodities that serve as consumer goods but that also have appreciation potential could be a source of significant capital gains. Owner-occupied housing, fine art, antique cars, or jewelry, for example, are often bought not only for current use but also for possible capital gain. Such gains should not escape tax. But the procedures proposed for ordinary investments assets would not work here, because the taxpayer would not be allowed to deduct the original cost of the jewelry, art, or owner-occupied housing. Hence, only the excess of the sales price over the purchase price, adjusted for inflation, should be taxed. For example, if a person buys a painting for $10,000, holds it for ten years during which prices double, and sells it for $35,000, tax should be imposed on the gain of $15,000, where the gain is calculated as $35,000 less $20,000 (the purchase price of $10,000 adjusted for inflation between purchase and sale).

Post-secondary Education

The cost of post-secondary education is a major investment and entails large cash outlays. Both characteristics raise important issues under the cash flow income tax. If expenditures on post-secondary education are regarded as investments, they should be deductible, because the income flow generated by the investment—increased future earnings—will be taxable.[25] Loans to finance such education would then be taxable receipts, and repayments of principal and interest would be deductible.

This approach would raise serious practical problems, however. First, much of the cost of higher education pays for amenities that do not add to future earnings. These costs should not be deductible. Furthermore, it would be hard to distinguish between post-secondary education that adds to future earnings and educational activities with a large consumption element. How, for example, would one treat the tuition charged for an art-study cruise in the Mediterranean? If this example seems extreme and the answer obvious, consider what the answer should be if the student is a museum curator. Second, if tuition at private universities is

25. Outlays on primary and secondary education are also investments in human capital. But neither the student nor the student's family pays for most of the costs of public education, other than food and lodging. Instead they are supported by government expenditures, which in turn are covered by taxes. It is impractical to permit parents a deduction for taxes they pay to support the schooling of their children, however, as most of the cost of such education is borne by others.

deductible, an inequity would be created for students in public institutions. Such institutions are supported out of tax payments, none of which would be deductible. In view of these problems and the fact that the cost of post-secondary education is not currently deductible under the personal income tax, we propose that no deductions be allowed for the costs of post-secondary education under the cash flow income tax.

This policy would raise other difficulties, however. First, it would still be necessary to identify bona fide training expenditures by employers (investments), which would be deductible by employers and not taxable to employees. Inevitably, the tax authorities would be forced to draw debatable distinctions, as they must under current law. Second, to prevent the bulge of outlays for higher education from pushing taxpayers into higher brackets, it would be necessary to permit parents to average self-financed costs for post-secondary education. This end could be reached through ten-year averaging, the same approach we suggest for gifts and bequests. In addition, parents or students could be permitted to exclude proceeds of loans for higher education from their tax base; but if they exercised this option, payments of principal and interest would not be deductible.

Trusts, Gifts, and Bequests

The taxation of gifts and bequests is essential to the cash flow income tax. If people were able to escape tax on such wealth transfers, the cash flow tax would be converted from a tax on lifetime income to one on consumption.

Trusts

Trusts permit taxpayers to surrender control over assets permanently or temporarily. The income from these assets may be taxed separately. If the surrender is temporary or revocable at the taxpayer's discretion, the assets continue to belong to the taxpayer, and no wealth transfers occur. For purposes of the cash flow income tax, the receipts flowing from such trusts should continue to be grouped with other receipts of the creator of the trust. Trust receipts paid to anyone other than the spouse of the trust creator would be regarded as taxable gifts.

If the trust is irrevocable, the taxpayer under the cash flow system has made a wealth transfer if total gifts exceed the lifetime exemption of $100,000 per person. Any payments from the trust would enter the tax base of the recipient. When the trust is terminated and the property is distributed, the recipients of this property, called remaindermen, would include the property in their tax base. Heirs would face no tax until they consumed their inheritances or transferred them to others.

Estate or gift taxes are generally imposed when wealth is transferred from one generation to another. People have long tried to avoid one or more rounds of estate or gift taxes by establishing generation-skipping trusts. Estate taxes are imposed only when the trust is created. But the payment of income, usually to children, and the subsequent distribution of the principal to future generations occasion no further estate or gift tax.

To prevent gross avoidance of estate and gift taxes, most states require the distribution of all property in a trust no later than twenty-one years after the death of the last person alive when the trust was created. Also, in 1976 Congress enacted legislation to discourage generation-skipping trusts. Despite such limitations trusts may last for many decades.

To minimize the use of the generation-skipping trusts to avoid the cash flow income tax, we suggest that a special tax be imposed every thirty years on the assets of trusts created after 1976. The tax would be imposed at the maximum personal tax rate of 32 percent except on trusts whose only remaindermen are the spouse or children of the creator of the trust. Such a rule would eliminate essentially all opportunities for using trusts to avoid tax. In this situation, people could avoid the tax on trust assets by giving the assets directly to living grandchildren or great-grandchildren. However, the thirty-year rule would not interfere with the use of trusts for reasons other than tax avoidance.

Gifts

The proper treatment of gifts depends on the nature of the asset. The treatment of gifts to trusts was just described. Other gifts would fall into one of three categories: cash, consumer durables, and investment goods.

Under the cash flow income tax, cash gifts enter the tax base of the donor as a use of resources, and they enter the tax base of the recipient as a receipt. If the gift is saved, the recipient would pay no tax until the cash was spent or given away. Enforcement of this tax poses special problems because of the difficulty of tracing gifts of cash and resulting consumption. Similar problems arise under the existing estate and gift taxes.

The gift of all other goods would produce the same tax consequences as if the donor had sold the goods and given away the proceeds. If the gift is an investment asset that had received qualified account treatment, its entire value would enter the tax base of the donor. The same value would also enter the tax base of the recipient, but there would be no tax liability due from the recipient until the asset was sold and the proceeds consumed or given away.

The gift of consumer durables, jewelry, art, or a house that the donor had occupied would require different treatment. Only the real (inflation-adjusted) appreciation of the asset since purchase would be included in the donor's tax base, because the donor had not previously deducted the purchase, and hence had paid tax on it. The full value of the gift would be included in the recipient's tax base because the gift is a consumer good, unless the recipient chose to sell the asset and save the proceeds.

Bequests

Bequests pose the same problems encountered under the current estate tax: how to value assets for which no market price is readily available and how to arrange deferred payment schedules when the estate is illiquid. Current law contains workable but overly generous procedures for dealing with these problems. They need to be retained but tightened. As noted earlier, averaging arrangements should be available for bequests that would otherwise push the taxpayer into higher tax brackets.

The most serious problems would arise from techniques currently used to avoid estate and gift taxes that could be carried over to the cash flow tax system. For example, a taxpayer can create a corporation with two classes of stock, preferred stock owned and voted by the taxpayer and nonvoting common stock, which is given to the taxpayer's children. Initially, all income of the corporation is paid to the preferred share-holder. The common stock is given a low value, because it receives no dividends and has no voting rights. Hence, little or no gift tax is due. But all growth accrues to the benefit of the common shareholders. The value of the stock in the parent's estate is frozen because the preferred dividends are frozen, and the children enjoy any increase in the corporation's value free of estate tax.

Another avoidance technique is available to landowners. They may divide large holdings into checkerboard parcels and give undeveloped alternating parcels to their heirs. The value of the gift is relatively low because the land is undeveloped. Then the parents can develop the parcels they retain. If such investments are successful, they will boost the value of neighboring land as well. This increase in value accrues to the original owner's heirs free of gift or estate tax.[26]

Opportunities to avoid tax with these devices and others like them would have to be severely curbed under the cash flow income tax. In some cases, a change of law would be easy to enforce, in others, extremely difficult. In the case of each of the avoidance devices described above, it would be necessary periodically to reexamine the valuation previously placed on gifts. In some cases, the final revaluation might occur at the time of the donor's last tax return.

No set of rules will forestall all tax avoidance or evasion through unrecognized gifts or bequests. Nor would it be possible to avoid all inequities. For example, gifts of a costly education would not be subject to gift tax. Parents might share vacations with children or provide them free or low cost access to a summer house. But most wealth transfers can be adequately taxed if Congress writes the necessary laws, Treasury issues the necessary regulations, and the courts enforce them.

International Migration

Special problems arise because of international migration. Consistent rules must be designed for taxing movements of wealth into or out of the country.

If transfers of assets from the United States by emigrants were ignored under the cash flow income tax, almost unlimited opportunities for tax avoidance would be created. People with accumulated assets would

---

26. In his *A Voluntary Tax? New Perspectives on Sophisticated Estate Tax Avoidance* (Brookings, 1979), George Cooper vividly describes these and other techniques in the text. Authors have yet another tax avoidance device. They may give typescripts of their new books to heirs. The courts have judged that such gifts are merely bundles of paper and are therefore of negligible value. The heir receives all royalties on the book free of gift or estate tax.

have a strong incentive to emigrate to countries with lower taxes on the use of resources for purposes of consuming their wealth or transferring it to others. To minimize this incentive, tax should be imposed on cash flow out of the United States. This goal could be achieved by requiring that all qualified accounts be held at institutions resident in the United States and that a withholding tax be imposed at the maximum personal tax rate on all transfers from such accounts to persons or businesses not resident in the United States. People leaving the United States would be able to defer tax on accumulated assets by leaving them in such accounts.

Immigrants should not have to pay tax on wealth brought into the country, however. Forcing them to pay tax might result in double taxation, because such assets may have been accumulated after paying taxes under other tax systems. Such assets, therefore, could carry with them a deduction against current or future taxable cash flow equal to the taxpayer's basis in the assets or the fair market value of such assets on date of entry.

Foreign investments of U.S. individuals would be treated in most respects like domestic investments. Taxpayers would be allowed deductions for such investments, and they would be required to include in the personal tax base all cash distributions from these investments.[27]

State Income Taxes

Forty states now impose general personal income taxes. Thirty-two of them refer to specified items from the federal personal income tax, and some require the taxpayer to do little more than copy various lines from the federal tax return. Even in states with income tax systems that do not refer to the federal return, taxpayers are able to use many personal records for both state and federal returns.

The same information about earnings would be required for the cash flow income tax and the present annual income tax, but the treatment of capital transactions would be quite different. The cash flow tax would not require information on reinvested capital income, depreciation, capital gains, or other transactions that now give rise to various credits and deductions. Until states integrate their personal taxes with the

27. To prevent U.S. residents from evading tax on accumulations of such assets by leaving the country, deductions for investments in such assets should be allowed only if the taxpayer placed them with institutions maintaining qualified accounts.

federal cash flow income tax, taxpayers would have to compile such information for state tax returns.

The incentive would be strong for states to convert their tax systems to the cash flow basis and to spare taxpayers the need to collect such information. In addition, to the extent that the cash flow system broadens the tax base and represents a federal commitment to refrain from additional major changes in the tax code, states would be further encouraged to follow the federal lead.

Transition

Many people hold assets accumulated out of income on which personal income tax has already been paid. If people sold these assets to finance consumption or wealth transfers after the advent of the cash flow income tax, a second tax would be levied on the resulting cash flow unless special rules discussed in this section were provided to prevent double taxation. The rules would require no record keeping beyond that now required for calculating capital gains.

No income tax has been imposed on many existing assets. Qualified pension plans, stocks purchased at low cost but with high market value, property which has been fully depreciated, and tax-sheltered savings accounts are all low or "zero-basis" assets, which means that all or almost all proceeds from the sale of such assets are taxable under current law. They would also be fully taxable under the cash flow income tax. In contrast, many other assets, such as bank accounts, most stocks and bonds, and newly purchased depreciable property, are high-basis assets. For such assets, owners are normally entitled under current law to recover their costs without paying additional tax. This section shows how, under the cash flow income tax, owners could continue to recover the costs of such assets held when the new system comes into effect.

To facilitate exposition, the date of adoption of the cash flow income tax will be referred to as "T day." Preexisting assets and liabilities are those held by the taxpayer before T day.

The transition rules for assets and liabilities acquired before T day can be considered separately. Additional rules may be needed for special circumstances.

Assets

Taxpayers may deduct the basis of preexisting assets sold after T day. This rule allows taxpayers to recover fully the adjusted basis (original cost less depreciation) of assets acquired before T day. It requires no calculations of net worth or total basis when the new system takes effect. Instead, basis can be determined as each asset is sold. This procedure does not require any calculations other than those required under current law to compute capital gains. As is the case for newly acquired assets, gross proceeds from the sale of preexisting assets would be included in the cash flow income tax base.

Basis of assets sold after T day should be increased from T day until the asset is sold, with the increase based on a market rate of interest. Without this rule the present value of preexisting basis would decline as time passes. This adjustment eliminates this incentive to sell preexisting assets for tax reasons immediately after T day.

The basis of preexisting assets not deducted from the cash flow income tax during the taxpayer's lifetime can be added to the $100,000 estate and gift exemption. This rule assures taxpayers that they will not be doubly taxed whether they consume preexisting assets or transfer them to others by gift or bequest. It would also reduce the tax collected at death for the first generation subject to the new regime. This rule eliminates after one generation any tax-motivated reason for keeping track of the basis of assets.

Liabilities

Deductibility of interest on preexisting loans would cease on T day. Standard treatment of loans under the cash flow system includes borrowing in the tax base and deducts repayments of principal and interest. An alternative treatment, equal in present-value terms to the standard treatment, allows borrowing to be excluded but denies deductions for repayments. Because preexisting loans never entered the tax base, the denial of interest deductions after T day provides all such loans the equivalent of the standard loan treatment. The standard treatment would apply to all loans after T day, including loans that may be obtained to pay-off existing loans.

Advantages of the Transition Rules

The asset and liability transition rules are symmetric. They convert assets and liabilities to full cash flow treatment promptly on T day. The cost of preexisting assets not recovered under the income tax is immediately deductible (in present-value terms) against the cash flow tax, just as if this cost had been incurred under the new regime. Disallowing interest deductions on outstanding loans treats loans as if the unpaid balance had been incurred under the cash flow income tax.

The immediate denial of interest deductions on all preexisting loans, even those that may have been incurred only shortly before T day, may appear harsh. Because most debt is incurred to acquire assets, however, the combined effect of the asset and liability rules is symmetric and approximately offsetting. For example, if the loan balance and basis of an asset bought with the proceeds of the loan are equal, the transition rules are perfectly coordinated in present value terms. Unless tax rates change, the loss from denial of the interest deduction exactly matches the gain from the nontaxability of the return on the asset. Where the basis of assets is greater (less) than the value of outstanding loans, the taxpayer gains more (less) from the deductibility of basis than he or she loses from the denial of interest deductions.

Although not so readily apparent, the transition rules are also even handed for taxpayers with outstanding loans and fully depreciated (zero-basis) property. Such taxpayers, who have negative net worth in accounting terms, seem to receive no compensation for the loss of deductibility on outstanding loans. This view is superficial, however. To amortize the principle of the loan, the borrower must use part of the gross flow from the fully depreciated asset. Under the annual income tax, this gross return would be fully taxable even though interest would be deductible. Under the cash flow income tax, the denial of the interest deduction would be matched by the nontaxability of the gross return as long as the funds are used to repay the loan or are otherwise invested. Again, the treatment of assets and liabilities is equivalent.

For a taxpayer with no assets and only preexisting liabilities, the equivalence breaks down. In practice, however, it is hard to imagine circumstances under which a taxpayer will have significant liabilities, no assets, *and* legitimate interest deductions.

These transition rules deal with the primary carryover issue under the cash flow income tax—the elimination of double taxation for assets accumulated under the income tax and consumed under the cash flow tax. They are designed to minimize the opportunities for anticipatory portfolio manipulations that might benefit the taxpayer and reduce short-run revenue flows.

The recovery of basis, with interest adjustments after T day, assures that no benefit in present-value terms results from the sale of assets, before or just after T day, followed by deductible reinvestment of the proceeds. Similarly, the denial of interest deductibility on preexisting loans gives taxpayers no incentive for anticipatory borrowing before T day.

Supplementary Rules

Despite the above rules, there are reasons to expect that the double deductions associated with recovery of basis and investment of the proceeds of asset sales could have serious short-run revenue effects. For example, taxpayers interested in rearranging their portfolios may wait until after T day to avoid possible capital gains taxes on assets sold under the income tax rules. After T day, offsetting sales and purchases would have no effects on cash flow income tax liability. Of perhaps greater importance, immediately after T day, some taxpayers may want to realize deductions by selling high-basis assets and reinvesting the proceeds. Taxpayers might follow such a strategy either because deductions are worth more to them currently than are the same deductions plus interest in the future, or because they doubt the survivability of the cash flow income tax. In these circumstances, supplementary transition rules are required to prevent a short-term drop in revenue, even though the present value of revenues is unaffected.

Either of two alternative supplementary rules would maintain short-run revenue flows:

The reduction in a taxpayer's cash flow income tax liability resulting from deductions for the recovery of basis on preexisting assets cannot exceed some fixed percentage (say, 50 percent) of the liability that would otherwise be due. The disallowed deductions would be carried forward with interest for five years and would be fully deductible against future tax liabilities after that time. If the taxpayer dies before five years have passed, the deferred deduction could be taken against the tax base in the year of death.

A deduction is deferred for a proportion (say, 50 percent) of the modified basis of preexisting assets sold in any tax year. Modified basis is equal to the basis of preexisting assets sold, times a fraction the numerator of which is gross proceeds from the sale of preexisting assets and the denominator of which is net asset purchases in the period. The deferred deduction would be carried forward with interest but could not be taken until five years had passed or in the year of the taxpayer's death, if sooner.

These two rules both maintain short-run revenues, but they operate differently. The first rule maintains the tax base whether or not the proceeds from the sale of preexisting assets are reinvested or consumed. The second rule defers a portion of the deduction for the recovery of basis to the extent that preexisting assets are liquidated and reinvested instead of consumed. The second rule comes into effect only when double deductions would otherwise be claimed. If preexisting assets are liquidated for consumption purposes, none of the proceeds from their sale are used to purchase other assets, and the second rule as a consequence would not be invoked. This rule is, therefore, less likely than the first to affect older taxpayers who sell assets to maintain consumption.

Neither rule affects the present value of tax liabilities, apart from possible changes in marginal tax rates. If this issue is of concern, it is possible to operate each rule as a special tax rather than as the denial of a deduction. In the first case the base of the special tax would equal the basis of preexisting assets sold during the year, and in the second case it would equal the modified basis (as defined) of such assets. The tax imposed each year at some moderate rate (perhaps 15 percent) would be carried forward with interest and would be creditable against future cash flow income taxes.

APPENDIX B: CALCULATION OF THE CORPORATE CASH FLOW TAX RATE

THE CORPORATE TAX BASE under the cash flow tax contains two elements: (1) the withholding tax base, which equals payments of dividends, interest, rents, and royalties paid abroad by U.S. firms and (2) the cash flow attributable to the excess of inflows to firms, excluding issuance of stock, over outflows on wages, materials, and investments.

The Withholding Tax Base

Data published by the Internal Revenue Service on payments subject to withholding taxation under current law provide a starting point for estimating the size of the withholding tax base. Interest and dividends paid abroad amounted to $10.6 billion in 1982, based on the most recent tax returns filed for withholding taxes (form 1042S). This amount is more than twice the $5.0 billion paid only three years earlier, in 1979.[28]

There are several reasons to believe that the potential tax base for a comprehensive withholding tax on payments abroad is far larger than $10.6 billion. First, much interest was exempt from withholding taxation in 1982. The Deficit Reduction Act of 1984 exempted even more, but the base was already severely eroded. Second, although not exempt by statute, some transactions are taxed lightly if at all because of tax-treaty provisions and the use of financial subsidiaries in tax-haven countries, especially the Netherland Antilles. In such instances, the quality of reporting of interest paid on form 1042S is likely to be poor because little or no tax is at stake. Third, even where withholding tax liabilities are of significance, compliance is likely to be spotty because of the ability of taxpayers to conceal the exact timing of payments abroad. For these reasons, a 50 percent expansion of the tax base under the cash flow tax, to $16 billion at 1982 levels, seems conservative.

Net Inflows

The base for the second element of the cash flow tax on corporations, net inflows of funds, can be estimated in one of two ways. The first follows from the definition of the tax base described in this chapter: the sum of receipts from such sources as the sale of products and services, borrowed funds net of principal repayments, and interest received net of interest paid; less costs of materials and supplies, labor, and capital goods. Alternatively, the tax base may be estimated as payments out of the corporation to its shareholders, net of funds received from shareholders through the issuance of new stock.

28. See Chris R. Carson, "Nonresident Alien Income and Tax Withheld, 1982," *SOI Bulletin,* vol. 4 (Fall 1984), pp. 21–32; and Carson, "Nonresident Alien Income and Tax Withheld, 1971–79," *SOI Bulletin,* vol. 1 (Spring 1982), pp. 34–38.

The equivalence of the two methods follows from the identity that all sources of funds to the corporation must equal all uses of funds. Sources of funds equal gross receipts plus net borrowing plus proceeds from stock issues; uses of funds equal costs of materials, wages, and capital investments plus net interest paid plus dividends paid. In terms of the two approaches to the cash flow tax base discussed here, the identity is as follows:

$$\text{(gross receipts)} - \text{(costs of materials, wages, and investment)}$$
$$+ \text{(net borrowing)} - \text{(net interest payments)}$$
$$\equiv \text{(dividends paid)} - \text{(proceeds from stock issues)}.$$

The left side of the identity is net inflows to the corporation, and the right side is payments to shareholders.[29]

To illustrate these relationships, take a simple transaction—a firm selling widgets and receiving an inflow of cash that can be either invested in assets of use to the firm or distributed as dividends to shareholders. If the cash is used to purchase other assets, nothing is added to the cash flow tax base under either measure. On the net inflow measure, the inflow of funds (gross receipts) is matched by a deductible outflow (cost of investments); on the basis of distributions to shareholders, there is simply no dividend paid in this case.

If the cash is used for a dividend distribution, the tax base is again the same under either measure, but now it is positive either because the excess of inflows of funds over deductible costs is positive or because there is a positive distribution to the shareholder. As long as proper account is taken of how the tax payments themselves are to be treated, the two tax bases are identical.

Calculating the Base

To simplify estimation of the corporation cash flow tax base, we have calculated this base as dividends paid minus proceeds from sale of stock. However, to put this base on the same before-tax terms as is used in calculating the current corporation tax base, we have added tax liabilities

---

29. For a discussion of the equivalence of these two approaches to cash flow taxation of corporations, see *The Structure and Reform of Direct Taxation*, pp. 227–68.

Table 4-5. *Corporate Cash Flow Tax Base of Nonfarm,*
Nonfinancial Corporations, 1981–83 Combined
Billions of dollars, unless otherwise specified

Item	Amount
1. Federal corporate income taxes	115
2. Net dividends paid	209
3. Issues of new shares	28
4. Net distributions to shareholders (line 2 less line 3)	181
5. Withholding tax base	49
6. Total cash flow tax base (line 1 + line 4 + line 5)	345
7. Corporate tax rate (percent) (line 1 ÷ line 6)	33

Source: U.S. Department of Commerce, Bureau of Economic Analysis, unpublished data; Board of Governors of the Federal Reserve System, flow-of-funds accounts.

as well.[30] The tax base is then the sum of current corporation taxes plus dividends paid to shareholders less proceeds from sale of stock.

We have made two other adjustments. First, we have calculated the base only for nonfarm, nonfinancial corporations. The tax base of financial institutions is hard to quantify precisely.[31] The best data come from the Federal Reserve Board flow-of-funds accounts, which employ the nonfarm, nonfinancial sectoral classification. Second, we have tried to equate revenues under the cash flow and annual corporation income taxes, not on a year-by-year basis but over a three-year period from 1981 to 1983. We use the longer period because annual corporation income fluctuates more than dividend payouts. As a result, a single year is likely to be unrepresentative of average conditions.

Table 4-5 shows the results. Federal corporation tax liabilities for nonfarm, nonfinancial corporations were $115 billion for the three years 1981–83 combined. For the same set of corporations, net dividends paid amounted to $209 billion, and new shares issued were $28 billion, yielding net payments to shareholders of $181 billion. We estimate the potential withholding tax base to be $49 billion over the three-year period. Thus,

30. A tax rate can be calculated as a tax-inclusive rate, R_i, where R_i equals tax liabilities divided by the tax base; or as a tax-exclusive rate, R_e, where R_e equals tax liabilities divided by the base minus tax liabilities. If the rate is defined consistently, the same dollar amount of taxes is raised regardless of the base. That is, $R_i = R_e/(1 + R_e)$, or $R_e = R_i/(1 - R_i)$.

31. On the basis of limited data, the ratio of current-law tax liabilities to the cash flow tax base for a portion of the financial sector—an aggregate consisting of commercial banks, mutual savings banks, credit unions, and savings and loan associations—appears to be roughly the same as exists for nonfinancial corporations.

the combined tax base is $345 billion, three times the actual tax liabilities of nonfarm, nonfinancial corporations for 1981–83; a tax rate of 33 percent would, therefore, raise the same revenue as was raised in 1981–83 by the current corporation and withholding taxes on these firms. This rate is approximately the same as the top personal tax rate, 32 percent.

CHAPTER FIVE

Sales Taxes

SALES TAXES in one form or other are receiving increasing scrutiny in the debate on reform of the federal revenue system.[1] Proposals to increase federal reliance on indirect taxes have focused on two types of levies—general sales taxes and selective taxes on energy. Supporters of a nationwide general sales tax recommend either a federal retail sales tax or a value-added tax. Surveys usually report that sales taxes are less unpopular than other taxes,[2] but only state and local governments have traditionally used retail sales taxes in the United States. The other form of general sales tax—the value-added tax—is levied at each stage of the production process. Although it is almost untried in the United States, it is used extensively by nine member-countries of the European Community, where it accounts for an average of 17 percent of government revenue, and by many other nations as well.[3]

Production or use of energy is the most frequently mentioned target for increased excise taxation by the federal government. An energy tax might be imposed only on imported energy products in order to reduce

1. Sales taxes in the form of excises provided only 5.6 percent of federal revenues in 1984, and under current law this share is expected to decline to 3.1 percent in 1990. State and local governments, however, derive more than one-third of their revenues from sales and excise taxes. See Congressional Budget Office, *The Economic and Budget Outlook: Fiscal Years 1986–1990* (CBO, February 1985), table E-3. As noted in chap. 3, the U.S. Treasury Department in November 1984 proposed a major tax reform based on a vastly improved income tax. In a companion report issued at the same time, however, it also found merit in the value-added tax, although its advantages were found to be insufficient to justify its use "merely to reduce reliance on the income tax." See U.S. Department of the Treasury, *Tax Reform for Fairness, Simplicity, and Economic Growth: The Treasury Department Report to the President,* vol. 3: *Value-Added Tax* (Treasury Department, 1984), p.1

2. Advisory Commission on Intergovernmental Relations, *Strengthening the Federal Revenue System: Implications for State and Local Taxing and Borrowing,* Report A-97 (Washington, D.C.: ACIR, 1984), p. 3.

3. Henry J. Aaron, ed., *The Value-Added Tax: Lessons from Europe* (Brookings, 1981), p. 14.

reliance on foreign supplies. Or it could be imposed on all energy wherever produced. In both cases, the motivation for the tax is dual— to collect more revenues and to discourage energy consumption.

Value-Added and Retail Sales Taxes

The value-added tax is a sales tax levied at each stage of production on "value added," the difference between total sales proceeds of businesses and the cost of goods and services purchased from other firms. The invoice or credit method of paying the tax is the form most widely discussed in the United States and most commonly used abroad. Under this method the firm determines the tax liability due on its sales, takes a credit for the tax (stated on its invoices) already paid by its suppliers of materials and capital goods, and remits the net amount to the Treasury.[4]

A value-added tax that excludes investment goods from tax is equivalent to a tax on all consumption and has the same economic effects as a truly comprehensive retail sales tax.[5] The value-added and retail sales taxes have several similarities. First and most important, they can produce a lot of revenue—an estimated $12 billion to $16 billion per percentage point of tax in 1986 and $15 billion to $20 billion by 1989 (see

4. An alternative approach is directly to calculate value added and then pay the tax based on this calculation. To illustrate how this direct approach—or subtraction method— would work, assume that a tax of 10 percent is imposed on all value added. A firm has gross receipts of $100 during the taxable period. During the same period it spent $57 on purchases from other firms, $28 on wages and salaries, and $8 in interest payments and made a profit of $7. That firm's value added under this subtraction method is $43 ($100 minus $57) and the firm would be required to pay tax of $4.30. Under the credit or invoice approach discussed in the text, the firm could be charged a tax of 10 percent of its gross sales, or $10, and allowed a credit of $5.70 for taxes paid by its suppliers. The amount of tax is the same, but administrative procedures are sensitive to which approach is used. A comprehensive 10 percent retail sales tax could yield the same amount of revenue as the value-added tax. Firms with no retail sales would be exempt, but all consumption is reflected in retail sales. At the point of final sale to consumers, a tax of 10 percent of all consumption would be collected, the same result as under the value-added tax.

5. The total of all payments to factors of production is gross national income at factor cost. Gross national income, by definition, equals gross national product at factor cost. GNP is the sum of consumption, investment, government spending, and net exports. If net exports and government spending are not subject to value-added tax and if investment is deductible, the tax falls only on consumption.

Table 5-1. *Calculation of Base for a Consumption-Type Value-Added Tax, 1982*
Billions of dollars

Category	Value
Total consumption expenditures in GNP	$1,992
Maximum feasible VAT	1,773[a]
Potential VAT base, after probable exemptions	1,462[b]
Minimum VAT base	1,070[c]

Source: Advisory Commission on Intergovernmental Relations, *Strengthening the Federal Revenue System,* Report A-97 (Washington, D.C.: ACIR, 1984), p. 70.

a. Total consumption less rental value of homes and farms, foreign travel expenditures (net of expenditures in the United States by foreigners), and religious and welfare activities; plus monetary interest paid by individuals.

b. Probable exemptions: medical care (hospitals and health insurance), local transportation excluding taxicabs, clubs and fraternal organizations, parimutuel net receipts, private education and research, services furnished without payment by financial institutions, food furnished by employers, handling cost of life insurance, rent for tenant-occupied nonfarm dwellings, domestic service.

c. Potential VAT base less food purchased for off-premises consumption and medical care other than hospitals and health insurance exempted above.

table 5-1).[6] With an unlimited vista of federal budget deficits of $200 billion or more, this characteristic is appealing. Second, both the retail sales and value-added taxes are favored by those who wish to tax consumption and exempt capital income or to shift from personal to commodity taxation. The value-added tax in particular has long been regarded by some as a possible substitute for less well regarded taxes such as the corporation income tax.[7] In addition, advocates point out that comprehensive consumption taxes do not disturb household choice among consumption goods. However, every country with a value-added tax, every U.S. state with a retail sales tax, and every proposal for one of these taxes at the federal level excuse many consumer goods and services from the tax. Certain commodities are likely to be relieved of some or all tax for one of three reasons: to reduce tax burdens on low-

6. These estimates have been calculated by extrapolating the potential and minimum value-added tax bases shown in table 5-1 to the years 1986 and 1989 under the assumption that the 1982 ratios of the two bases to GNP remain unchanged. For GNP projections to 1986 and 1989, see the Congressional Budget Office, *The Economic and Budget Outlook: Fiscal Years 1986–1990* (CBO, 1985), table I-10. The net revenue estimates in the text also assume a 20 percent reduction in income tax receipts as a result of the value-added tax. Given GNP at market prices, income tax collections fall because the imposition of the value-added tax reduces factor incomes.

7. The Committee for Economic Development two decades ago called for replacing the corporation income tax with the value-added tax. CED, *A Better Balance in Federal Taxes on Business* (New York: CED, 1966), p. 10. More recently, Al Ullman, former Chairman of the House Ways and Means Committee, proposed using a value-added tax for reducing payroll and other taxes. See Aaron, ed., *The Value-Added Tax,* p. 1.

income groups; to simplify administration; or to encourage the consumption of particular goods.[8]

Distribution of Tax Burdens

A comprehensive value-added tax at uniform rates would be regres-
sive (tax low-income groups proportionately more than high-income
groups) with respect to annual or lifetime income, because the share of
income that is saved rises with income.[9] Most countries with a value-
added tax have tried to reduce this regressivity by excusing necessities
from full taxation. In some countries this policy has made the value-
added tax roughly proportional to annual income.[10] Most states with a
retail sales tax exempt such consumer goods and services as food,
housing, education, and professional services.

Administration and Coverage

A truly comprehensive value-added or retail sales tax would pose
serious administrative problems because it is hard to value some activities, such as services rendered by financial institutions and nonprofit
organizations and the imputed rental services of owner-occupied housing
and other durable consumer goods. To avoid these problems, all existing
value-added tax systems exclude some kinds of consumption from the
tax base.

Not taxing all consumption reduces some administrative burdens,
and imposing low rates on goods consumed disproportionately by low-

8. Relief is usually provided by imposing a reduced tax rate on the favored item.
The most favorable treatment is a zero rate. Under this arrangement, firms are taxed
at the low rate on their gross sales and are permitted to deduct taxes paid at the normal
or higher rate by their suppliers. Taxing a commodity at a low or zero rate is more
favorable than exempting the good altogether, because exemption prevents the firm
from claiming credit for value-added taxes paid by its suppliers. See note 4 above for
an explanation of the value-added tax mechanism.

9. Available data show conclusively that the fraction of income consumed falls as
annual income rises. Data also suggest that consumption is proportional to income
averaged over many years, but these income data do not include accruals of capital
gains. See, for example, Franco Modigliani and Richard Brumberg, "Utility Analysis
and the Consumption Function: An Interpretation of Cross-Section Data," in Kenneth
K. Kurihara, ed., *Post-Keynesian Economics* (Rutgers University Press, 1954), pp. 388–
436; and Milton Friedman, *A Theory of the Consumption Function* (Princeton University
Press, 1957).

10. Aaron, ed., *The Value-Added Tax*, p. 14.

income households reduces regressivity. But these gains are not purchased without cost. The existence of many categories of commodities
with varying rates of tax creates opportunities for avoidance and adds
to the complexity of compliance and enforcement. Even deciding the
category to which a particular commodity belongs can be alternately
vexing and amusing.[11]

Certain goods and services are taxed lightly because such consumption is viewed as meritorious, regardless of the financial circumstances
of individual consumers. Fiscal authorities could easily tax such commodities as education or medical care, for example; but they usually
forbear because they do not wish to discourage their use.

Broad value-added taxes could cover about 90 percent of consumption, which is somewhat more than half of GNP; narrow ones would
cover about half of consumption, which is roughly one-third of GNP
(see table 5-1).

Evaluating a Broad Sales Tax

A broad sales tax would impose significant tax burdens on those now
regarded as having too little income to pay income taxes.[12] Congress
could offset such burdens by providing refundable personal income tax
credits to an estimated 55 million people in households that do not pay
any tax.[13] Providing credit, in addition, to those who now file but who
pay only a small part of income in tax would require millions of additional
rebate payments. The result would be increases in the cost of income
tax administration and compliance. Furthermore, payment of such
rebates would raise the rates necessary to meet any revenue target.

11. For example, in France, books and nonpornographic entertainment are taxed at
a reduced rate, recording equipment and pornographic entertainment at an increased
rate; radios are taxed at the increased rate, while television sets are subject to the
normal rate. See Jean-Pierre Balladur and Antoine Cautière, "France,"in ibid., pp. 19–
29. In the United Kingdom the purchase tax (replaced by the value-added tax in 1973)
applied to silverware and fur coats at the maximum rate and household textiles at the
minimum rate; ice cream and chocolate biscuits were subject to tax while smoked
salmon and caviar, along with smoked cod and cod roe, were all exempt. See Richard
Hemming and John A. Kay, "The United Kingdom," in ibid., pp. 75–89.

12. Some low-income earners now actually receive subsidies, because they pay little
or no income tax and qualify for the earned income tax credit, a tax benefit provided
to many persons with earned income below $11,000 per year and payable in cash if the
credit exceeds taxes otherwise due.

13. Estimate based on simulations from the Brookings tax model.

Sales and value-added taxes receive mixed marks for efficiency. Like the cash flow income tax but unlike the present annual income tax, they are free of the bias against future consumption. But advocates are wrong when they claim that a value-added or retail sales tax would not distort consumption choices, because all such taxes in fact fall unevenly on different forms of consumption and are therefore distorting.

More important than any such distortions is the fact that imposing a sales tax, broad or narrow, does nothing to correct the inefficiencies generated by the existing personal and corporation income taxes. Of course, revenues from the value-added tax could be used to reduce income tax rates. But unless Congress corrects the shortcomings of the income tax directly, imposing a value-added or retail sales tax would only add a new tax with new distortions to an old tax with old distortions.

The introduction of some form of sales tax would produce an important side effect. If wages and profits initially stay the same, the price of taxed goods and services would rise by the amount of the tax. Automatic cost-of-living adjustments could trigger subsequent wage increases, which would lead to further inflation. If the monetary authorities tried to prevent inflation by restricting the growth of the money supply, some drop in real demand for goods and services would occur unless wages and profits immediately fell enough to accomodate the new tax. Since wages in most industries rarely fall, the entire short-run brunt would fall either on payments to capital, hence impairing investment incentives, or on the demand for labor, hence causing unemployment. In either case it seems likely that the monetary authorities would let prices rise, causing at least a temporary jump in inflation.

Some claim that value-added taxes would make the American economy more competitive in world markets, because unlike income taxes, value-added taxes are rebated on exports and imposed on imports. If prices rise by the amount of the tax, however, prices of exported goods will not change, and imports will bear the same tax as domestically produced goods. Even if prices rise less than the amount of the tax, there is no reason to expect any long-term impact on the competitiveness of American industry under a system of floating exchange rates.

On administrative grounds, sales taxes have both virtues and short-comings. Experience from Europe indicates that the value-added tax works, although not without administrative problems.[14] The retail sales

14. For a discussion of administrative problems, see Sijbren Cnossen, "The Netherlands," in Aaron, ed., *The Value-Added Tax,* pp. 51–53.

tax also works well in the United States, although significant problems arise in classifying goods and in distinguishing between retail and other sales. Problems with cross-state sales that plague state adminstrators would not occur under a national tax.

Implementation

A national value-added tax would require a wholly new administrative apparatus for which neither the Internal Revenue Service nor any other federal agency now has the staff. A new staff, estimated to number about 20,000, would have to be hired and trained.[15] Businesses would have to be educated about the new tax and would have to organize their accounts to comply with it. Individuals would have to familiarize themselves with the tax as well and be prepared to accept the probable increase in retail prices when the tax takes effect.

Experience from Europe suggests that a value-added tax could not be implemented in the United States in less than two or three years. Most European countries had broad commodity taxes in place before they enacted the value-added tax, but they still took eighteen months to two years to implement it. A national retail sales tax could probably be implemented more quickly if the federal government used state sales tax administrators as its agents. Such an arrangement would probably work best if the federal rate were set high enough not only to meet federal revenue requirements but also to replace state sales taxes.

State and Local Opposition

A federal retail sales or value-added tax would create at least one serious political problem. In the view of many, it would hinder state and local governments from raising retail sales taxes and might make it difficult for states to retain them. Value-added tax rates could be set high enough not only to meet federal revenue goals but also to permit the federal government to "buy out" the retail sales taxes of states and localities. Under such a scheme a portion of tax proceeds would be used to provide grants to states, in return for which the states would give up retail sales taxation. Based on state and local government collections from general sales taxes in 1984, 5.5 percentage points would have to be

15. Treasury Department, *Tax Reform*, vol. 3: *Value-Added Tax*, p. 1.

added to a federal tax to replace those revenues.[16] But it is unlikely that the states would willingly surrender their fiscal autonomy in such a swap. In addition, the bases of state sales taxes vary greatly, with some states imposing tax on, and others exempting, sales of food, clothing, restaurant meals, professional services, gasoline, and other items. Because a federal tax base would be uniform across the states, many states would have to accept a much wider or narrower tax base than they now use.

Pitfalls of Exempting Retail Sales

To reduce the anticipated resistance by state and local officials to a federal value-added tax, some people have suggested that the tax should not be imposed at the retail stage.[17] Since states tax retail sales, it is thought that they would be less concerned if a federal tax omitted that stage of business.

This way of dealing with one political drawback of the value-added tax would create potentially serious distortions. The first arises because the importance of retail sales varies greatly from product to product. Value added at the retail stage is only a small part of the retail price for such items as food or automobiles. For other items, such as restaurant meals, beauty parlor services, and personal legal or medical services, value added at the retail stage is a large part of the price. It is not clear why the tax system should favor commodities with a lot of value added at retail over commodities with little value added at that stage.

In additon, exempting the retail stage would encourage economically unsound efforts to minimize tax. For example, retail establishments might try to avoid tax by producing inputs it formerly bought from other companies. To make matters worse, exemption of the retail stage would be difficult to enforce, especially on vertically integrated companies, such as Sears, Roebuck and Company, that manufacture items for sale in their own retail stores. To determine how much value added takes place at each stage, a "price" must be set at which goods are transferred

16. State and local general sales tax collections in 1984 were $75 billion. See Advisory Commission on Intergovernmental Relations, *Significant Features of Fiscal Federalism, 1984–85* (Washington, D.C.: ACIR, 1985), tables 30 and 39. These collections are equal to 5.5 percent of the average of the potential and minimum value-added tax bases shown in table 5-1, as extrapolated to 1984.

17. See Charls E. Walker, *The Case for Fundamental Tax Reform: Questions and Answers,* Special Report (Washington, D.C.: American Council for Capital Formation, 1984).

from manufacturing to the retail stage. Where a single firm is the manufacturer, wholesaler, and retailer, these prices are arbitrary, and the firm has every incentive to set them to minimize taxes. Tax collectors would have to decide how much value was added at retail and how much at earlier stages, an inherently arbitrary exercise. The alternative of imposing no tax at all on sales by vertically integrated retailers is clearly discriminatory. There is no easy way to administer a tax that exempts the retail stage, despite the sharp reduction in the number of small firms on which the tax is imposed.

In short, the proposal to exempt the retail stage under a value-added tax would introduce distortions, reduce economic efficiency, and complicate administration for vertically integrated firms. It has no appeal except as a political ploy to fool state and local officials about the true nature of a value-added tax. Whether it would succeed even in this objective is unclear. As noted above, the bases of a retail sales tax and an ordinary value-added tax are formally identical.[18] Exempting the retail stage reduces a realistic value-added base by about 15 percent nationwide.[19] The great bulk of the economic overlap remains.

The Hall-Rabushka Plan

As noted earlier, value added for each firm equals total receipts minus the cost of investments and supplies. Value added can be divided into two components: (1) wages and salaries paid to employees of the firm and (2) a residual equal to total business receipts less wages and salaries, investments, and supplies. The second component could be termed "cash flow profits," the surplus of cash inflows over outlays in the current period.

Based on this distinction between wage and nonwage value added, Robert E. Hall and Alvin Rabushka have proposed a variant of the value-added tax as a replacement for the current individual and corporation income taxes. Senator Dennis DeConcini (Democrat of Arizona) first

18. See note 4 above.

19. For 1982, national income in retail trade, computed without adjusting capital consumption allowances for consistent accounting for replacement cost, amounted to $206 billion. See *Survey of Current Business,* vol. 64 (July 1984), table 6.3B. To convert this figure into an estimate of the value-added tax base in retail trade requires a net adjustment for the excess of depreciation allowances used in deriving this income figure over total investment made by the retail trade sector in 1982. This net adjustment has a slight negative value, yielding a value-added base of about $205 billion, or 14 percent of the potential value-added tax base shown in table 5-1.

introduced legislation embodying their proposal in the 97th Congress.[20] The Hall-Rabushka plan would tax wages at the household level and the rest of value added at the business level, all at the rate of 19 percent. They claim that this rate would yield approximately the same revenue as the current personal and corporation income tax.

There are some important differences between the Hall-Rabushka plan and the conventional value-added tax. First, the taxation of wages at the household level permits personal allowances to be deducted from the tax base. For 1985, for example, Hall and Rabushka would allow personal deductions of $4,500 for single taxpayers and $9,000 for joint taxpayers, plus $1,800 for each dependent. A family of four could thus earn $12,600 before paying the wage tax. Such personal exemptions ameliorate much of the regressiveness of the value-added tax, because those with little wage income and no other resources would not be subject to tax at all. Under Hall-Rabushka, there would be no personal tax on capital income or transfer payments such as social security, welfare, and unemployment insurance.

Second, taxing earnings at the household level allows the Hall-Rabushka tax to be more comprehensive than a conventional value-added tax for two reasons. (1) The Hall-Rabushka plan would tax earnings in government and the nonprofit sector as well as earnings in private industry. In contrast, most value-added taxes do not reach value added in the government and nonprofit sectors. (2) Because of the tax-free range under the Hall-Rabushka plan, there is little justification for exempting specific commodities to help low-income households. Personal exemptions more effectively reduce tax burdens on low-income households than do exemptions of particular categories of consumption.

Third, the Hall-Rabushka plan would not tax exports and imports in the same manner as under most value-added taxes. Ordinary value-added taxes are rebated on exports but are imposed on imports. These rules constitute the principle that all goods bound for the same destination should receive the same tax treatment. In contrast, the Hall-Rabushka plan, which has no mechanism for rebating taxes on exports or for imposing taxes on imports, is based on the origin principle—all goods originating in the same place should be taxed identically.

Despite its personal exemptions, the Hall-Rabushka plan would

---

20. Robert E. Hall and Alvin Rabushka, *Low Tax, Simple Tax, Flat Tax* (McGraw-Hill, 1983); and Hall and Rabushka, *The Flat Tax* (Stanford, Calif.: Hoover Institution Press, 1985). The bill was reintroduced in the 99th Congress on January 31, 1985, as S. 321.

redistribute tax burdens to the benefit of the well-to-do and against middle-income families. High personal exemptions protect low-income households, but the flat rate sharply reduces taxes for high-income households, despite the broadened tax base. Since revenues are unchanged, the taxes previously paid by the well-to-do must be paid by the middle class. The Hall-Rabushka plan, in common with other forms of consumption tax, does not reach receipts from gifts and inheritances, as a result, it does not tax all sources or uses of lifetime resources.

Relationships among Tax Plans

The Hall-Rabushka plan helps illustrate the close resemblance between value-added and income and hence between value-added taxes and income taxes.[21] Through a series of changes, an ordinary value-added tax can be converted into a progressive annual income tax or a progressive cash-flow income tax. By including personal exemptions, the Hall-Rabushka plan takes the first step toward converting the value-added tax into a close relative of the annual income tax. Two additional changes would complete the process: the single 19 percent rate could be replaced with graduated rates on earnings, and the provision allowing the immediate deduction of the full cost of investments by businesses could be replaced by deductions based on true economic depreciation. The resulting system, unlike a progressive annual income tax, would tax all capital income at a single rate only at the business level. Progressivity would be maintained because of personal exemptions and the graduated rate structure on wage income and, with a sufficiently high flat rate on capital income, because of the increasing share of capital income as income levels rise.

If the immediate deduction of the cost of investments were retained and the household tax base were expanded to include inheritances, the resulting tax would be similiar to the cash flow income tax described in chapter 4. In contrast to the cash flow income tax, which falls on all uses of resources, the Hall-Rabushka plan as modified in this way would fall on all sources of income; but, as noted in chapter 2, these two tax bases are alternative ways of measuring income.

21. This section draws heavily on informal conversations with David F. Bradford, former deputy assistant secretary for tax policy and currently professor of economics at Princeton University.

The relationships among the bases of the various plans suggest that it is possible to design plans that embody some elements of each. The mix-and-match strategy carries the grave danger, noted in chapter 2, that incompatible principles may be combined, as they are under current law. The problems created by tax-sheltered saving juxtaposed with deductions of interest payments are illustrative. But it is important to understand that other coherent plans can be fashioned from the elements of the plans described in this book.

Summary

A national value-added tax cannot begin to yield significant revenue until perhaps three years after it is enacted. A national retail sales tax might be placed in operation somewhat more quickly, but only if the federal government used states as administrative agents. In that event, rates would almost surely have to be set high enough to buy out existing state retail sales taxes. After implementation, however, either a value-added or a retail sales tax would be powerful revenue raisers that could play a large part in a long-run program to reduce the deficit.

With the exception of the Hall-Rabushka proposal, which would replace the existing personal and corporation income taxes, a value-added or retail sales tax would not relieve Congress of the obligation to correct the unfairness, distortion, and complexity arising under the current personal and corporation tax system. Only changes in the personal and corporation taxes themselves can solve these problems. Neither a value-added nor a retail sales tax can achieve a fair, efficient, or simple tax system unless it is combined with direct reforms of personal and business taxes.

Energy Taxes

Federal and state taxes on energy long predate the energy inflation of the 1970s. States impose severance taxes on the value of oil, gas, and coal produced within their borders. Both the federal and state governments collect excise taxes on gasoline and certain other fuels as an indirect charge on highway users. In 1980, after the second round of OPEC-induced increases in petroleum prices, Congress imposed a windfall profits tax on domestic producers of crude oil in an attempt to tax the gains from a jump in their sales prices in excess of increases in their production costs.

New proposals and increased taxes on energy are now under discussion for at least three reasons: the need for additional revenues, the recognition that domestic energy resources are limited, and the continuing dependence of the United States on foreign suppliers. To reduce the role of foreign suppliers, some propose a $10-per-barrel tax on imported petroleum and petroleum products to raise the price of imported petroleum and indirectly increase the price of all domestically consumed petroleum products. The price increase would encourage individuals and businesses to switch to other forms of energy and to undertake research on how to use energy efficiently. At the same time, a tax on imported petroleum would increase domestic production. Such a tax would also increase revenues $19 billion annually when fully effective.[22] Opponents have pointed out that additional production would speed the depletion of domestic petroleum reserves; that other ways to reduce dependence on foreign petroleum are available, such as building up the strategic petroleum reserve; and that the price increase from a tax on imports, like the initial increase in energy prices, would generate windfall profits for domestic producers.

A tax on petroleum and petroleum products—whether produced abroad or in the United States—would meet some of the objections to a tax on imports alone. It would raise even more revenue than a tax only on imports, an estimated $44 billion at $10 per barrel;[23] it would not generate windfall profits for domestic producers; and it would encourage the development of alternative energy sources. But it would discourage additional domestic petroleum production and, therefore, would not reduce imports as effectively as a tax limited to imports.

Some have proposed a tax on all nonrenewable sources of energy. A 10 percent tax on the value of all energy consumption—from petroleum, coal, natural gas, and nuclear power—would raise about $33 billion per year.[24] Such a tax would reduce total energy demand more effectively than would taxes at an equivalent rate on petroleum alone. But it would

22. Congressional Budget Office, *Reducing the Deficit: Spending and Revenue Options* (CBO, 1985), pp. 238, 239–40. The revenues estimated for this and other proposals discussed in this section assume an effective date of January 1, 1986. Estimated revenue increases for fiscal 1986 are about 70 percent of those for fiscal years 1987–90. These estimates are all net of reductions in other taxes.

23. Ibid., pp. 238–39.

24. Ibid., pp. 238, 242.

be less effective than the alternatives in reducing current dependence on imported petroleum.

The choice among energy taxes clearly depends on the relative importance of reducing current imports of petroleum, reducing the depletion of U.S. reserves, or overall conservation of other types of energy. But all energy taxes have important shortcomings as elements of a program of tax reform. First, they all would increase tax burdens on households regarded as too poor to pay income taxes. No roster exists of low-income taxpayers whose energy expenses would qualify them for assistance. Developing and maintaining such a roster would be costly and cumbersome. Passage of a program of low-income energy assistance that is both effective and manageable seems improbable. Second, energy taxes will boost energy prices, which in turn will lead to increased general inflation unless monetary and other economic policies prevent it by slowing overall economic activity. Thus, energy taxes are likely to increase either inflation or unemployment. Third, energy taxes, except for possibly reducing marginal tax rates, do nothing directly to correct the existing tax distortions and inequities in the personal or corporation income tax system.

Summary

The principle appeal of general sales or selective energy taxes is that they can raise a lot of revenue although, in the case of value-added taxes, not very soon. But they leave the shortcomings of the existing tax system uncorrected, and they have their own serious problems of fairness and efficiency. In short, they do nothing to improve the quality of our tax system. They can help close the deficit in the long run but only if Congress is prepared to shift tax burdens to lower income groups or to implement administratively cumbersome schemes to offset such a shift.

CHAPTER SIX

Short-Run Programs
for Raising Revenue

THE STRUCTURAL tax reforms discussed in chapters 3, 4, and 5 would take time to achieve. But the federal deficit, which in large measure is focusing congressional attention on the revenue system, demands prompt attention. Congress may, therefore, choose to follow a two-track strategy, passing a tax increase as one element of a program to reduce the deficit while proceeding more deliberately on fundamental tax reform. In this chapter we examine four ways to increase taxes that would not require extended debate. We judge each program by its prospects for prompt enactment and its consistency with the tax principles presented in chapter 2. The four proposals presented here are representative of the short-run tax plans Congress is likely to consider.

Criteria for Short-Run Tax Increases

By our definition, a good short-run tax increase would be easy to enact and, at a minimum, would not hinder structural tax reform. The programs examined below differ in both dimensions. Although all could be enacted and implemented within one year, some will be harder to enact than others.[1] Also, some programs modestly reform the tax structure and others do not. But none would hinder adoption of the annual income tax plans described in chapter 3 or the cash flow income tax described in chapter 4.

As noted in chapter 1, taxes must be raised by about $100 billion in fiscal year 1989 to close one-half of the budget gap. Rather arbitrarily,

1. The revenue estimates presented here assume all proposals have an effective date of January 1, 1986, yielding less than a full year of revenue gain for fiscal 1986 (ending September 30, 1986).

we stipulate that a short-run program must generate at least half of these revenues, $50 billion by fiscal year 1989 (about 0.9 percent of GNP). By comparison, the Deficit Reduction Act of 1984 increased taxes $17 billion in fiscal 1986 and will raise about $25 billion annually (or 0.5 percent of GNP) for each of the next three years when fully effective.[2] Thus, although the short-run programs presented here supply only half of the revenues needed by 1989, each raises twice as much as the 1984 act.

The Four Programs

Table 6-1 presents the revenue gains from four short-run tax programs. Plan A is an across-the-board increase in all corporation and individual income taxes, achieved through either a 9 percent surcharge on all tax bills or a 2.2 percentage point addition to all marginal rates. With a 9 percent surcharge, the lowest bracket would increase from 11 percent to 12 percent, the top rate from 50 to 54.5 percent, and the top corporate rate from 46 percent to 50.1 percent (that is, the rate rises by 9 percent in each case). Therefore the surcharge would increase all tax liabilities proportionately. Alternatively, an increase in all marginal tax rates by 2.2 percentage points would yield the same total revenue as a 9 percent surcharge but would be less progressive.[3] Both approaches raise taxes most on those who currently pay the most tax.

Plan B would broaden the tax base instead of boosting rates. As proposed by Representative Fortney H. (Pete) Stark (Democrat of California), it would scale back itemized deductions by 10 percent and virtually all other tax preferences by 20 percent.[4] This proposal cuts a wide swath, ranging from a stretch-out of the recovery period for depreciation to a cutback of mortgage interest deductions. Like plan A, plan B is an across-the-board approach, intended to diffuse opposition

2. For estimated budget effects of the act see *General Explanation of the Revenue Provisions of the Deficit Reduction Act of 1984*, Committee Print, prepared by the Joint Committee on Taxation, 98 Cong. 2 sess. (GPO, 1985), table 1. For estimated GNP, see ibid., table I-11.

3. Going from 11 percent to 13.2 percent in the lowest bracket is a 20 percent increase in liability, whereas a rise from 50 percent to 52.2 percent for the top bracket is only a 4.4 percent increase.

4. Legislation to this effect was introduced in the 99th Congress by Representative Stark as H.R. 1377 on February 28, 1985. On the same date, similar but not identical legislation was introduced in the Senate as S. 556 by Senator John H. Chafee (Republican of Rhode Island).

Table 6-1. *Revenue Gains from Four Short-Run Tax Proposals,*
Fiscal Years 1986 and 1989
Billions of dollars

Proposal	Fiscal year revenue gain	
	1986	1989
Plan A		
9% surtax on individual and corporate tax liabilities	39	52
Plan B		
Across-the-board base-broadening	8	45
Plan C		
Selected rate increases	13	50
1. High income: 10% surtax	2	7
2. Corporate: 10% surtax	7	13
3. Modification of indexing	4	30
Plan D		
Combination plan	26	51
1. Specific base-broadening measures	15	34
a. Repeal of state sales tax deduction	6	8
b. Limitation of interest deduction	*	3
c. Taxation of portion of employer-provided health and all life insurance premiums	7	16
d. Full basis adjustment for investment tax credit	1	5
e. Extension of recovery period for structures to 20 years	*	2
2. Excise taxes	6	7
a. Doubling of taxes on beer and wine	1	1
b. Continuation of 16-cent tax on cigarettes	2	2
c. Increase of gasoline tax by $0.05 per gallon	3	4
3. Delay further indexing (after 1985) until Jan. 1, 1987	5	10

Source: Congressional Budget Office, *Reducing the Deficit: Spending and Revenue Options* (CBO, 1984), pp. 182–243; and *Reducing the Deficit* (CBO, 1985), pp. 53, 225–307. Revenues from the extended recovery period for structures are based on estimates given in *General Explanation of the Revenue Provisions of the Deficit Reduction Act of 1984*, Committee Print, prepared by the Joint Committee on Taxation, 98 Cong. 2 sess. (GPO, 1985), table 2.
* Less than $0.5 billion.

by treating all tax preferences uniformly.[5] In sharp contrast to plan A, however, it increases taxes most for persons who currently benefit most from tax preferences.

Plan C, like A, would increase rates, but unlike A, the increases would be larger for high-income than for low-income taxpayers. Plan C resem-

5. If the economic life of asset A is the same as the depreciable life under current law, while the economic life of asset B is twice the depreciable life, then a 20 percent lengthening of depreciable lives—the approach taken in the Stark bill—is a move toward accuracy in the measurement of income for asset B and away from it for asset A.

bles the tax plan proposed by Walter Mondale during the 1984 presidential election campaign. It consists of two elements: a 10 percent surcharge aimed at upper-income taxpayers and a partial suspension of indexing. The surcharge would be applied to corporations and high-income individual taxpayers—joint filers with incomes of more than $100,000 and single filers with income of more than $70,000. Indexing would be modified but in a way that prevents bracket-creep for low-income taxpayers. For example, indexing could be allowed only for personal exemptions and the zero-bracket amount but not for other tax brackets. This approach would keep many low-income families off the tax rolls and sustain most benefits of indexing for most families who remain subject to tax. Alternatively, indexing could be limited to the excess of inflation over, say, 3 percent. This approach would uniformly reduce the benefits of indexing.

Plan D is a grab-bag in the tradition of the Tax Equity and Fiscal Responsibility Act of 1982 and the Deficit Reduction Act of 1984. It would raise taxes by a variety of measures with no single theme. Plan D selectively broadens the income tax base, increases selected excise taxes, and suspends indexing for 1986. It would repeal itemized deductions for state sales taxes, would limit all itemized interest deductions to net investment income plus $10,000 for a joint return ($7,500 for other returns), and would repeal the exclusion of employer-provided term life insurance premiums and part of health premiums (the amount in excess of $175 per month for family plans or $70 per month for single plans). Also, it would permit taxpayers to depreciate only the excess of equipment costs over the investment tax credit, and it would stretch out depreciation for structures.

Evaluation

Short-term packages are appealing only because the deficit requires immediate action. However, some short-run approaches are more likely to contribute to sound structural changes than others. How well do these four proposals stack up?

Prospects for Short-Term Enactment

No short-term tax program can be enacted unless both Congress and the administration recognize the urgency of increasing revenues. Even if this condition is met, these four proposals do not have equal chances of enactment.

Plan A is simplest, but it would provoke two kinds of opposition. First, even a temporary increase in rates aggravates current distortions. Second, a surcharge seems unfair because it adds most to the burdens of those who already pay most tax under current law. The only legitimate counter argument to this criticism is that the need for revenue is too urgent to permit lengthy debates about structural reforms. This argument can be persuasive, however, only if the surcharge is believed to be temporary; that is, if the commitment to structural reform is widely accepted and the prospects for enacting such reforms—and repealing the surcharge—are good.

Plan B also embodies the across-the-board principle, but it should appeal to tax reformers more than A, because it falls more heavily on taxpayers who benefit disproportionately from itemized deductions, credits, allowances, and other special provisions. However, as always, cutbacks of tax preferences will be strongly resisted, a serious drawback if quick enactment is the first priority. Furthermore, the apparent evenhandedness of this approach may disguise quite different impacts across activities. Like plan A, therefore, it too may have a higher likelihood of enactment if regarded as part of a longer-run effort.[6]

Plan C would increase some rates more than others. Not only does it increase the effects of distortions in the tax base, as does A, but it also undoes in part what many regard as the most significant structural change in recent years—indexing of tax brackets and personal exemptions. Furthermore, abandonment of the across-the-board approach might retard enactment. A debate on how tax burdens should be distributed is not a prescription for quick tax action. As with plans A and B, considering proposal C as just the first step in a more fundamental tax restructuring could brighten prospects for its acceptance.

Plan D is certainly the most conventional program, but that is no guarantee of greater acceptability. Congress has often considered and equally often rejected all of the specific base-broadening measures in plan D. Other provisions could be substituted for them, but most alternatives have a similar history. Excise taxes on beer and wine would match increased taxes on distilled spirits enacted in 1984. The excise tax on cigarettes, now 16 cents per pack, is scheduled to fall to 8 cents per

---

6. Long-run reform is in fact the clear objective of its sponsor, Representative Stark, because as drafted the proposal would terminate in 1989.

pack on October 1, 1985. Sustaining the current rate should prove more acceptable than many alternative revenue-increasing measures. Boosting gasoline taxes may be more difficult politically and would not reduce the deficit if the receipts were deposited in the highway trust fund and led to increased outlays on highway construction. A one-year suspension of indexing could be defended on the ground that prices have risen less than anticipated since 1981, when tax rates were reduced; as a result, there has been less bracket creep and, hence, a larger tax cut than most members of Congress expected. Proponents of indexing may strongly resist even a temporary postponement, however, fearing that it will be the precursor to repeal. Past experience with suspensions of enacted reforms amply justifies this view.[7]

If the plans were seen as temporary measures certain to be followed quickly by structural reforms, we would rank plan A most likely to succeed, followed closely by B and C, with D a distant fourth. In contrast, if these proposals were seen as likely to remain in effect for many years, the likelihood of enactment would change markedly, indeed even reverse. Plan D would then become most acceptable and A least acceptable as a permanent change in the tax code. But if any tax change is regarded as permanent, the legislative infighting would be fierce and hence the prospects for swift action greatly diminished.

This is yet another illustration of the link between short-run revenue needs and longer-run structural reform. Tax reform takes time; revenues to help close the deficit are needed urgently. The chance of quickly increasing revenue depends critically on whether the program is seen as a temporary bridge to thorough tax reform or as a permanent change in the system. The objectives of both long-run reform and short-run tax increases are best served by clearly identifying any action as an emergency response to current revenue needs.

7. Perhaps the most prominent example is the provision enacted in the Tax Reform Act of 1976 for the carryover of the basis of inherited assets. This provision would have required persons inheriting property with accrued but unrealized gains to carry over the basis or cost of these assets from the decedent so that whenever the asset was subsequently sold, all gain—even that accruing during the lifetime of the decedent— would be taxable. Prior law would have allowed the heir an increase in the basis of such assets to the market value at time of the decedent's death. Thus, accrued but unrealized gains during the decedent's life would never be taxed. After enactment, the provision was first suspended and then repealed in the Windfall Profit Tax Act of 1980. Another prime example is withholding of interest and dividends, enacted in 1982 and repealed, before becoming effective, in 1983.

Contributions to Structural Reform

As to the implications for long-term reform, we ask two questions of each plan: (1) Is it itself a reform measure? (2) Will it serve the purposes of long-run reform?

Plan B ranks highest on both counts. Although billed as temporary, it would directly limit many tax preferences and indirectly promote a thorough review of the system. Such a review could well lead to fewer preferences and lower tax rates along the lines of the long-run proposals examined in chapter 3. Although plan D also contains some base-broadening elements, it only slightly reverses the erosion of the tax base and is certainly not of a scale sufficient to permit lower marginal tax rates.

Plans A and C contribute nothing directly to structural tax reform. At best, they serve to maintain pressure for more fundamental changes in the future.

Summary

The lessons for both the short run and the long seem to coincide. The best hope for dealing with both the deficit and the defects of the current tax structure is to tie together in a single commitment, if not a single legislative package, a temporary across-the-board tax increase in the style of plan A or B and long-run reforms that offer the promise of reduced marginal tax rates.

CHAPTER SEVEN

The Politics of Tax Reform

IN PRIVATE, political leaders of both parties agree on many ways to make the tax system fairer, simpler, and more efficient. In public, however, few will acknowledge any sympathy for these same changes. Vigorous, intelligent, and well-paid lobbyists beset members of Congress with arguments that one particular tax provision or another is vital to the nation and that the campaign contributions over which the lobbyist has influence are vital to that member's reelection. The analytical issues about how *best* to reform the tax system are difficult, as preceding chapters illustrate, but the primary obstacle to making the tax system *better* is not a lack of agreement on things to do but of political will to do them. Only the president can successfully assert the broad public interest and create a shield behind which individual members of Congress can be protected from assaults of particular interests.

This chapter will explore the political roots of complexity, inefficiency, and favoritism in the tax system. The same political forces now arrayed against reform would try in the future to reinstate favoritism in a reformed tax code. In light of these forces, the chapter will describe the prerequisites for successful tax reform.

The Way We Are and How We Got That Way

According to the Joint Committee on Taxation of the U.S. Congress, the tax code contains more than 100 special deductions, credits, exclusions, amortization rules, and exemptions.[1] All were designed to achieve some worthy social or economic objective without adding to direct federal outlays. For example, when Congress wanted to help families

1. See *Estimates of Federal Tax Expenditures for Fiscal Years 1984–1989*, prepared for the House Committee on Ways and Means and the Senate Committee on Finance by the Joint Committee on Taxation, 98 Cong. 2 sess. (GPO, 1984).

bear the cost of child care, it did not provide direct payments to eligible families; instead it first enacted a deduction and later a credit for child care expenses. When Congress wanted to encourage rehabilitation of structures and reforestation, it did not create programs in the departments of Housing and Urban Development or Interior; it extended the investment tax credit to outlays for reforestation and rehabilitation. When Congress wished to promote state and local outlays to control pollution, it did not enact a new program of grants; it permitted pollution abatement facilities to be financed with tax-exempt securities. When Congress decided to compensate low-income families for the burden of social security payroll taxes, it did not provide such families with direct assistance; it enacted the earned income tax credit.

Other special tax provisions enacted during the last twenty-five years were designed to patch up defects in the basic tax system. Thus, the accelerated cost recovery system enacted in 1981 was intended in part to offset the loss in value of depreciation deductions caused by inflation. The exclusion of interest on certain savings certificates and the expansion of individual retirement accounts were proposed to encourage saving. And the provisions for accrual taxation of futures contracts were designed to reduce the use of futures contracts to avoid tax on other income. As noted in chapters 2 and 3, however, there are many other such distortions that cannot be so easily avoided under the current tax system. In addition, the side effects of such partial and piecemeal cures have often proved to be as debilitating as the illness.

These examples could be extended manyfold. They illustrate four central propositions. First, the objectives sought by most of these special provisions are not frivolous. To the contrary, most were intended either to advance important social and economic objectives, such as cleaning up the environment and helping second earners enter the labor force, or to correct fundamental deficiencies in the tax structure, such as preventing inflation from discouraging investment.

Second, many of these objectives could have been achieved by direct expenditures or governmental regulations. Direct expenditures, however, would increase the *apparent* size of the federal government. The fact is that tax concessions increase the deficit at least as much as equally effective direct outlays. Indeed, tax concessions usually spill even more red ink than direct outlays do, because concessions are harder to confine to specific purposes or narrowly defined groups. Nonetheless, only direct spending is perceived to increase the size of government, although both approaches have this effect. Accordingly, tax concessions have an important political advantage over direct spending even when direct outlays are cheaper, more efficient, and more equitable. Direct expenditures also seem to require more government administrators than do tax provisions. But, as noted in chapter 2, this difference often reflects the willingness of Congress and the American public to accept standards of administration for tax programs that would not be tolerated for direct outlays.

Third, the desire of the public and of Congress to hold down direct federal spending will not end even if Congress enacts sweeping tax reform. It will continue to encourage the uses of tax concessions rather than direct outlays to achieve worthy objectives. The current effort to cut government spending will only reinforce this tendency.[2]

Fourth, the benefits from most tax provisions are concentrated on a small minority of all taxpayers. In contrast, the large costs of these concessions—the increased tax rates required to raise a given amount of revenue and the resulting distortions, the added complexity in filing tax returns, and the general perception of unfairness—are diffused widely and are therefore small for each person. The costs of lobbying are sufficient to discourage slightly injured people or businesses from troubling to make their views known. But beneficiaries with strong common interests find it worthwhile to pay lobbyists to represent their views, to form organizations to support particular tax provisions, and to make campaign contributions to compliant representatives and senators.

The same forces—the concentrated benefits and diffuse costs of tax favoritism—that produced the existing tax mess would make it difficult to sustain a coherent broad-based system if one were to be enacted. The same forces that gradually built the existing tower of confusion, exclusion by exclusion, deduction by deduction, credit by credit, will attempt to reconstruct a new edifice if the old one is torn down. Persuasive and well-paid advocates will present the case for just one more special

2. For symmetric reasons, one can expect that any successful program of base-broadening tax reform along the lines set forth in chapters 3, 4, or 5—with its attendant reduction or elimination of special deductions, credits, or exclusions—will increase the pressures for direct federal spending or regulation. See Robert W. Hartman, and Robert Lucke, "Aspartame for Comprehensive Taxation," paper prepared for the October 1984 annual meeting of the Association for Public Policy and Management.

provision for one more worthy cause as forcefully to Congress after reform as they did before. And each victory for favoritism paves the way for the next.

The power of special pleading to influence legislation is fueled by the dependency of elected officials on large campaign contributions by political action groups and individuals. The promise of campaign money in exchange for votes will not end merely because taxes are reformed; it will continue as long as congressional and presidential candidates depend on large campaign contributions.

For all of these reasons, tax reform will be exceedingly hard to enact and, if anything, harder to sustain.

Prerequisites for Comprehensive Tax Reform

The odds on achieving and maintaining a reformed tax system are long. But unless five conditions are satisfied, attaining this goal will be virtually impossible. These conditions are all-out presidential support, a single legislative bill, few floor amendments, awareness of a crisis, and provisions to ease transition.

Presidential Leadership

Fundamental restructuring of the tax system without fully committed presidential leadership is almost unthinkable. Only the president represents a national constituency. This political fact enables the president to speak for a broad national interest with less fear of retribution from important industries or demographic groups than members of Congress would have. Presidential candidates draw contributions from a wider range of groups and individuals than do candidates for lower office, and only presidential candidates receive a significant portion of the costs of running for office from public grants. A representative from a district dominated by the automobile industry will find it hard to vote to curtail deductions for consumer interest. A colleague from a district with a large university will find it hard to support any curtailment of the deduction for charitable contributions. Any elected official from Florida will find it hard to limit the extra exemption for the aged. And so it goes. A president is not immune to such pressures, but if so inclined can balance diverse and conflicting interests in developing a national program more readily than members of Congress can.

In the case of tax reform, the president must go well beyond ordinary backing of administration policy. The president must set the agenda on which Congress will have to act. And through the use of favors and the threat of vetoes, the president must actively shape the legislation that emerges from Congress.

One Comprehensive Bill

The essence of tax reform is the termination of many tax concessions all at once. This step would permit a large reduction in tax rates and considerably simplify tax returns and tax laws.

If only a few tax provisions are repealed at a time, only a small reduction in tax rates is possible without sacrificing revenue, and no appreciable simplification can result. In that event, members of Congress are placed in the difficult position of terminating provisions that were motivated originally by the desire to achieve some social or economic purpose, at a cost of potentially disruptive transitional adjustments, in order to achieve no compelling overall objective.

In some cases this strategy works. If the original motivation for a tax provision was based on fallacious reasoning, if the conditions that justified it have changed, or if the need for additional revenue is urgent, Congress may sometimes be motivated to act. In 1982 and again in 1984 the need to reduce the deficit drove Congress to enact a number of changes in the Internal Revenue Code that marginally improved fairness and efficiency. No simplification resulted from these tax bills, however, and both contained provisions that aggravated existing inefficiencies and inequities.

More fundamentally, the existing tax mess is the result of incremental tax "reform" enacted over a generation. Each succeeding Congress, responding to a different set of social and economic priorities and reflecting a different balance of political forces has enacted provisions that have considerable appeal in isolation but that add up to an incomprehensible and inconsistent melange. There is no reason to expect social or economic priorities to stop evolving or the ebb and flow of political fortunes to cease; therefore, there is no reason to expect a consistent and simplified set of tax rules to emerge from incremental tax reform.

For tax reform to have any chance of succeeding, the president must propose and Congress must confront a single, comprehensive bill, not a

series of partial and incremental changes. This strategic requirement
flows directly from the character of tax reform. A single, comprehensive
plan would permit the president and members of Congress to point to
large reductions in tax rates and major simplification to justify the repeal
of numerous narrow tax concessions. No special interest group could
claim that it was being singled out for punishment.

The need for a single bill does not imply that all reform provisions
must take effect at once. Individual provisions would, in all likelihood,
take effect at different times and many would be phased in gradually.
But unless all provisions are contained in the same bill, the promise of
rate reduction and simplification cannot be realized, and individual
groups will be able credibly to question why "their" tax advantages are
the ones singled out for repeal. There is no assurance that the strategy
of a single bill would succeed, but one can be confident that an incremental
strategy will fail.

One Vote

For a tax reform bill to succeed, amendments from the floor must be
held to a minimum. If floor amendments can be introduced freely, the
temptation will be overwhelming for each representative or senator to
try to protect tax provisions of particular benefit to their constituents.
Such votes would create the political situation that led to the present
predicament.

The best hope for restricting amendments lies in the careful working
out of all technical issues by the tax-writing committees in cooperation
with the administration so that a single "up-or-down" vote on the
resulting proposal can be taken by each house. The problems this
requirement presents in the House of Representatives are quite different
from those in the Senate.

Most floor votes in the House occur under specific rules voted by the
House Committee on Rules. These rules specify the time to be devoted
to debate and the number and range of amendments the entire House
can consider. Such rules are intended to prevent chaos in a large body
by assigning defined responsibilities to authorizing and appropriating
committees and by limiting the range of options that can be considered
on the floor. On some occasions the Committee on Rules specifies a
"closed rule," under which the entire House must vote without floor
amendment, on legislation reported out by other committees. This

procedure is used for particularly technical legislation or when the House leadership feels that a closed rule is the best political strategy. A "modified closed rule" specifies a limited number of defined amendments on which the House is permitted to vote. Comprehensive tax reform would be unlikely to succeed unless it were brought to the House floor under a closed rule or a modified closed rule. Without such a legislative procedure, floor amendments would almost certainly destroy any consistent approach embodied in legislation reported out of committee.

Senate procedures pose more serious obstacles. Senate debate is unlimited, and amendments on the floor are unconstrained unless at least sixty senators vote to limit debate. As a result, the full Senate has tended to enact tax legislation festooned with provisions that could not gain approval from its Finance Committee but that were added on the Senate floor during general debate. The number and variety of these tax baubles have led journalists and others to refer to tax bills passed by the Senate as "Christmas Tree" bills. Fortunately, many of the items added on the Senate floor are typically removed when conferees reconcile differences between Senate and House tax bills. It is reported that even the authors of some of the provisions added on the Senate floor do not expect or want them to survive and that Senate conferees, all of whom come from the Finance Committee, do not always fight vigorously to retain them. This traditional relationship underscores the importance of the House passing a bill that is as unadorned as possible.

Two recent legislative events give some hope that protection from amendment can be achieved in the House and Senate. In 1981 Congress voted a comprehensive Omnibus Budget Reconciliation Act, consisting of numerous and highly diverse elements, many of which called for large cuts in popular programs. Strong leadership in both houses, supported by the vigorous intervention of the newly elected President Reagan, sufficed to limit the number of amendments and secure an up-or-down vote on the bill as a whole. The procedure was defended on the ground that if many amendments were enacted, the initiative to cut spending would be dissipated by numerous small exceptions for programs dear to each representative or senator. Whether or not one agrees with the wisdom of the spending reductions, there is little doubt that the legislative procedure used to pass the bill helped achieve cuts that in many cases previous administrations had sought and failed to win.

A similar climate surrounded consideration of legislation enacted in 1983 to eliminate the deficit in the social security system. In May 1981

President Reagan proposed large cuts in social security. Sharp attacks led the president to create a bipartisan National Commission on Social Security Reform, chaired by Alan Greenspan, former chairman of the Council of Economic Advisers. To control the political damage from these attacks and find a compromise, the president instructed this commission to make its recommendations in December 1982, after the midterm congressional elections. The commission's recommendations were entirely satisfactory to few of its members but were acceptable to most and, as events subsequently revealed, to most members of Congress and to the president. The House Committee on Ways and Means made few changes to the proposal other than technical ones. The bill was sent under a modified closed rule to the House floor, where the full House accepted one major amendment, a gradual increase in the age at which unreduced social security benefits are first paid. The bill then passed. The Senate made no significant changes to the original proposal. Members of both houses resisted additional amendments on the ground that accepting them would cause the compromise to fall apart.

The critical issue is how to achieve similar discipline on tax reform legislation. As already noted, the possibility of such discipline without strong presidential leadership is remote. If the president had not made known his unwillingness to accept significant change to the 1981 budget reduction bill and the social security financing reform bill, Congress would not have been able on its own to resist such changes.

In the case of the social security amendments, an additional force was at work: Greenspan's commission. This commission reflected the positions of major interest groups with strong views on social security, including representatives of labor, manufacturers, insurance companies, and the elderly, as well as the leadership of both political parties. No significant opposition could be fielded against a plan acceptable to such a broad group and to the president. In effect the commission dulled the partisan edge of debate on the social security amendments and thus facilitated both compromise and enactment.

It is doubtful that a presidential commission could serve a similar role in fashioning tax reform. The number of interests is so large and diverse that no manageable commission could contain all politically influential views. No commission could quiet the lobbying or discourage the campaign contributions on which the numerous special provisions of the present tax system so much depend.

But there is a lesson to be learned. The crucial element is a political atmosphere in which the president and congressional leaders of both parties are seen as embracing a similar proposal and are thereby protected from partisan attack on the fundamental design of the program. Without vigorous leadership by the president as chief executive and leader of his party and without extensive consultation between the executive and legislative branches so that something close to one up-or-down vote can be achieved, no significant changes can be accomplished.

Crisis

Observers of congressional deliberations will realize that the suspension of political business-as-usual just described is rare except in time of crisis. A popular president would have to recognize the urgent need for tax reform, convince the American public of the urgency, and be willing to work with leaders of both parties in Congress. While such negotiations would be intensely political, partisan considerations would have to be muted, as they are during war or other national crisis, in recognition of an overriding national objective. Without this approach we do not believe tax reform can be achieved.

Unfortunately, the need for working in this fashion is usually difficult to demonstrate. If the economy is strong, the claim that tax distortions place the nation in jeopardy will be hard to sustain. Current conditions will seem to belie claims that the tax system retards economic growth and efficiency. When the economy is weak, in contrast, it will be difficult to argue that segments of the economy disproportionately aided by specific tax provisions, such as accelerated depreciation or consumer interest deductions, should be deprived of these advantages. The fundamental problem is that no time is ideal for tax reform. Those who would lose can always claim the national interest would be harmed if they were deprived of the special advantages they have enjoyed for so long.

Transition

The final prerequisite is careful attention to the problems of transition. Any program of comprehensive tax reform—a return to the principles of annual income taxation, a move to cash flow income taxation, or the adoption of a personal consumption tax—will deprive some businesses and individuals of important tax benefits. In chapter 4 we offered

solutions to several significant transition problems that arise from a shift
to cash flow income taxation. Similar problems would attend any other
comprehensive reform, and solutions would have to be devised.

A variety of transition steps can be added to any reform plan. Effective
dates can be delayed. Tax changes can be phased in gradually. "Grandfathering" may sometimes be appropriate. In some cases, direct federal
spending may be necessary to replace part of the benefits from existing
tax concessions.[3] In a few cases, it may be desirable to retain tax
concessions for specific activities within a reformed framework; in
chapter 4 we suggested some concessions for homeowners and for
charitable giving.

In all of these cases, transition rules to soften the harshness of tax
reform for those who lose tax advantages will for a time reduce some of
the gains in simplification. But without such transition rules, beneficiaries
of existing special provisions will be able to complain legitimately that
they are being asked unfairly to undergo shock therapy so that all may
enjoy a saner tax system. And the validity of that complaint would stand
as a major obstacle to achievement of a consensus for tax reform.

Conclusion

These prerequisites suggest that the best hope for tax reform is early
in the administration of a popular president; that is the time when he has
the prestige and political standing to push a comprehensive proposal
drafted in consultation with congressional leaders of both parties. The
president must communicate to the public his sense that tax reform is
important for the health and growth of the nation. Having hammered out
a compromise with congressional leaders, the president must make clear
that he will accept no major alterations and must use his powers to
secure support from members of his party.

Tax reform, therefore, is a high-stakes political gamble. Its supporters
must be willing to confront major economic and political interest groups,
each of whom will claim that, among all tax preferences, theirs should
be preserved. They must adhere to negotiated agreements enabling each
to state that seemingly meritorious exceptions cannot be allowed because

3. For example, in "Aspartame for Comprehensive Taxation," Hartman and Lucke
suggest a program of grants to people who are buying their first home.

they would jeopardize the greater good of comprehensive reform, lower rates, and simplification. Tax reform is possible only if all its supporters step forward together so that none can be singled out for political retribution.

Opportunities to achieve landmark reforms of the income tax are rare. Such an opportunity now appears to have arisen. The coincidence of the need to raise taxes to help balance the budget and of a widespread awareness that the tax system is unfair, inefficient, and needlessly complex has created this opportunity and, paradoxically, stands as a barrier to action. Many members of Congress want to lower the budget deficit with a combination of spending cuts and tax measures, but they understand that raising tax rates without reforming the base will aggravate existing distortions and inequities. Other members of Congress and the president believe that no increase in taxes should be considered until spending has been reduced as much as possible and prefer to cut spending enough to eliminate the need for any tax increase. This disagreement adds to the political barriers to tax reform. Only compromise, which by definition will please no one fully, holds out the promise of sustained and balanced economic expansion and greater fairness and efficiency throughout the tax system.

Index